D0052626

Outlaw Tales
of Colorado

Outlaw Tales of Colorado

True Stories of Colorado's Notorious
Robbers, Rustlers, and Bandits

Jan Murphy

TWODOT®

GUILFORD, CONNECTICUT
HELENA, MONTANA
AN IMPRINT OF THE GLOBE PEQUOT PRESS

To buy books in quantity for corporate use
or incentives, call **(800) 962–0973, ext. 4551,**
or e-mail **premiums@GlobePequot.com.**

A · T W O D O T® · B O O K

Copyright © 2006 by The Globe Pequot Press

All rights reserved. No part of this book may be reproduced or transmitted in any form by any means, electronic or mechanical, including photocopying and recording, or by any information storage and retrieval system, except as may be expressly permitted by the 1976 Copyright Act or by the publisher. Requests for permission should be made in writing to The Globe Pequot Press, P.O. Box 480, Guilford, Connecticut 06437.

TwoDot is a registered trademark of The Globe Pequot Press.

Cover design by Jane Sheppard
Cover photo: back cover (top) Denver Public Library, (bottom) Colorado Historical Society; front cover courtesy of the Denver Public Library.
Map by Stephen Stringall © The Globe Pequot Press

Library of Congress Cataloging-in-Publication Data
Murphy, Jan.
   Outlaw tales of Colorado: true stories of Colorado's Notorious Robbers, Rustlers, and Bandits/Jan Murphy.—1st ed.
       p. cm.—(Outlaw tales series)
   Includes bibliographical references and index.
   ISBN 0-7627-3789-1
   1. Crime—Colorado—History—19th century. 2. Crime—Colorado—History—20th century. 3. Criminals—Colorado—History—19th century. 4. Criminals—Colorado—History—20th century. I. Title. II. Series.
   HV6793.C6M87 2005
   364.1'09788—dc22

                                                      2005007681

Manufactured in the United States of America
First Edition/First Printing

For My Mother,
Joan Pierron Murphy

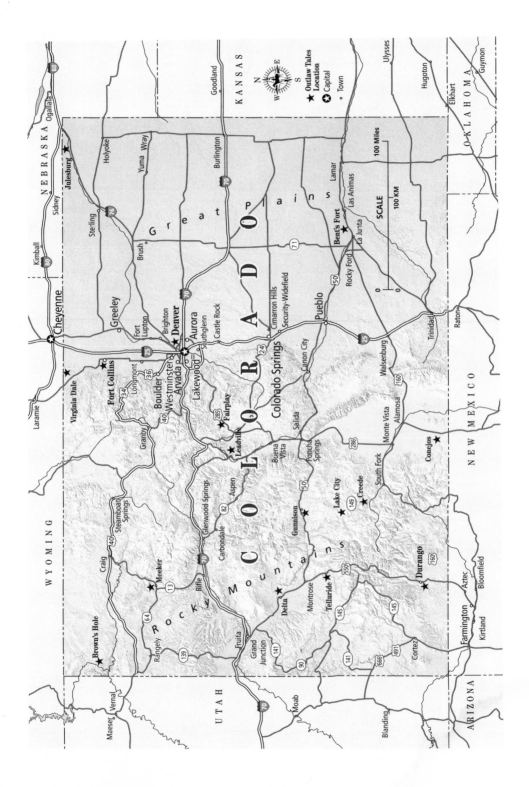

Contents

Acknowledgments

Writing may be a solitary effort but it does not happen alone. So I thank some of those who helped me:

The Jefferson County Public Library in Colorado for a remarkably comprehensive collection available for my research.

The Colorado Historical Society for help in acquiring photographs.

My editor, Stephanie Hester, whose calm, supportive guidance and direction were invaluable.

Those who offered special bits of information, insight, and suggestions for this book.

Kathy Zornes Samsel, for proofreading my proposal submission and for giving me good suggestions for this book, and for her longtime friendship beginning when we were freshman roommates at the University of Colorado at Boulder.

Carole Adams for giving me the computer I used to write this book.

Mabel Fry, of Clarkesville, Georgia. My dear friend.

Rosa Mazone, of the Universe. My mentor and guide, and friend.

Some other dear friends who have especially encouraged me, and cheered me on my way to, and during, the writing of this book: Karin Cooper, Katie Cooper, Cindy Millensifer, and Jan Pond.

My many relatives who include me in their lives, and have stuck with me through the years of my creative quests.

Also, my parents.

And my uncle, John Pierron.

And all those who sincerely and regularly asked, "How's the book coming?" and wanted to listen to the answer! You all know who you are! It meant a lot to me.

Introduction

There is no recorded history of outlaws in Colorado before the 1850s. Except for a few settlers and native tribes, no towns existed.

Colorado has one of the shorter recorded histories of the western states. Early explorers from Escalante and Dominguez to Fremont all reported this uncharted territory as having "mountains that are not climbable and land that is uninhabitable, except by the savage Indians." They were referring to the Rocky Mountains, which are higher in elevation in Colorado than anywhere else along its chain. They also found virtually no lakes or streams that held any appreciable amounts of water. As the United States of America expanded, all of the trails leading to the Pacific detoured around Colorado because of the impassable mountains and lack of water. Colorado would not become a territory until 1861, or achieve statehood until 1876.

The future site of the state of Colorado remained largely ignored. The California Gold Rush in 1849 caused only a tiny ruffle of speculation through Colorado. In 1850, there were so few non-native inhabitants that the main language spoken was Ute. The southernmost part of present-day Colorado had been sparsely populated in the 1700s under the flag of Mexico, whose government wanted their people to homestead the area. But the desolate land and lack of water discouraged most from settling. The name Colorado is of Spanish derivation and means "the color red"—named for the brilliant crimson hue of the soil.

Except for this small incursion, the native Indians still held forth as the primary population. Other than the predominant Utes, the other larger populations included the Cheyenne, Arapaho, Apache, and Kiowa. From 1833 to 1847 Bent's Old Fort was the only non-native outpost along the Colorado section of the Santa Fe Trail, which barely crossed into the southeastern corner of the present state.

The total region of modern Colorado sat mostly quiet and undisturbed, except for the occasional skirmishes between the native tribes. Even the native populations were said to number only in the thousands. Buffalo likely outnumbered people. This land was not only quiet; it was very, very empty.

The California gold rush began to play itself out and miners began to return from the far West to the Rocky Mountains. Gold had been found in a Colorado stream that gushed out of the mountains onto the plains, and a general excitement began to build. By 1857, a small town called Denver was chartered along the banks of Cherry Creek. Across from it, on the other bank, another town called Auraria began. Suddenly, as more gold and silver was found in "them thar hills," the population swelled. Adventurers poured in from every border. Lack of water and high mountains were no longer the formidable impediments they had once been considered. For riches, almost anything could be overcome. The gold diggers and silver miners who were rushing into this veritable vacuum were called the "59ers."

With this influx of fortune seekers, there were others who wanted to profit from these people's newfound wealth, and not always legitimately. Like parasites, some came to trick, rob, cheat, and steal from the hordes of men (and a few women) who had little bags of gold dust and silver nuggets stashed in their pockets (or in their petticoats). Others stole horses and cattle, money and jewels, and robbed banks, sometimes killing their victims.

Now, Colorado had outlaws.

Jack Slade, Gunslinger

There was such magic in that name, SLADE!" wrote author Mark Twain in his book *Roughing It*, an autobiographical account of his visit to the West as a young man.

While traveling toward the Rocky Mountains, Twain had been hearing about a certain man named Jack Slade. He was said to be a gunslinger, a killer who was feared by all. The conductors talked about Slade on the train, and the stories only grew more outrageous after the rails ended and Twain continued on by stagecoach.

Soon, Twain was so mesmerized by these tales that he wanted to hear about nothing else. What a land the West must be to have men like Slade roaming loose across the countryside. Twain's fertile imagination could only speculate as to what this man must be like.

Nearing Julesburg, in present-day Colorado, the stage passengers were hungry after traveling all night. They looked forward to giving their knotted muscles a rest from the bumpy and uncomfortable ride, and when the stage rattled on to the next station, they poured into the little building. Mark Twain sat down to breakfast at a table with the other passengers. Some Central Overland Company stagecoach officers, who were already there, joined the group. Twain was seated next to the superintendent, who was at the head of the table. He was a gentlemanly and mannerly fellow who was dressed better than the rest.

As they made introductions around the table, Twain realized the unfathomable. The superintendent was Jack Slade! Twain would later write, "Here, right by my side, was the actual ogre who, in fights and brawls and various ways, had taken the lives of twenty-six human beings, or all men lied about him! I suppose I was the proudest stripling that ever traveled to see strange lands and wonderful people."

Slade is believed to be the man on the left. His wife Virginia is sitting on the window ledge.
Montana Historical Society, Helena

Twain was both awestruck and fear-filled at the same time. He was having trouble matching this man sitting next to him with the one about whom he had heard so much during his travels. Indeed, Jack Slade was a complex character who had killed many men. He was employed by the Central Overland Company in the late 1850s to put an end to horse stealing at the Julesburg Station, but he clearly overstepped his calling on many occasions. Killing men, whether they deserved it or not, became a way of life. His eventual death by lynching would testify to his status as an outlaw. Yet many, like Twain, saw the side of Slade that was considerate and mannerly. His relationship with his wife Virginia, for instance, was a heartfelt union marked by deep caring and an abiding, gentle love—characteristics that were in sharp contrast to Slade's ever-developing reputation for violence.

Jack Slade was born on January 22, 1831 (some say it was 1829) just 40 miles east of St. Louis, Missouri in Carlyle, Illinois. This small city was located near other rural towns including Aviston, Germantown, St. Jacob, and Pierron, all of which had been founded by immigrants who were pushing the edge of civilization ever westward. Young Slade would grow up in this atmosphere of adventurers moving west.

Part of the enigma surrounding Jack Slade began in his childhood. He was the fourth of five children born to his parents, Charles Jr. and Mary Slade. Joseph Alfred Slade was his given name, but he was always called "Jack."

His father had founded the town of Carlyle in 1818, become its postmaster, and by 1832 was elected to the United States House of Representatives. Prior to this, he had been a United States Marshal and a member of the Illinois legislature.

Jack Slade's parents had power, wealth, and an esteemed reputation. But in 1834, when Jack was just a small child, his father died of cholera, leaving Jack with an unfillable void and a lack of a role model to guide his life. His mother married Elias S. Dennis just two years later, but the few early accounts of Jack's young life suggest he was an unruly child, and his mother complained of her inability to control him.

Jack was bright, educated in scholarly curriculum and mannerly decorum, and lacked for nothing material. Accounts of his boyhood say he was "capable of getting strait As in school," but there were also reports of his gradual inclination toward bullying and becoming a problem student.

When he was thirteen years old, the recklessness of his later life would be foretold in one brutal event. Historical accounts vary and inevitably mix fiction with fact, but even in general terms this event was an ominous sign of things to come.

It was summer in Carlyle when Jack and two other boys escaped their chores and met up in the shady comfort along the banks of the Kaskaskia River. Jack's buddies were from poor families with little education and unpromising futures. Most townspeople thought young Jack's choice of friends was not in keeping with his family background.

They had noticed that his actions and general demeanor seemed to "reek" of defiance.

On this day, a man emerged from the bushes along the bank. He was later identified as Mr. Gottlieb. Supposedly, he confronted the boys and threatened to disclose their participation in some illicit or ill-advised activity. It may have been for recent vandalism to his property, or possibly for catching them in the act of smoking as they sat there on the bank. Whatever it was, it was a challenge to the boys and it incited anger in young Jack Slade.

While the boys argued with Mr. Gottlieb, Jack was said to have positioned himself behind the man. He picked up a large rock and proceeded to bash Gottlieb over the head with it. Jack was apparently so enraged that he kept on hitting the man, smashing in his skull until Gottlieb was dead.

The boys all ran to their respective homes. The sheriff was supposedly called. But the story's facts are murky at best. One account says Gottlieb was a stranger in the area, and the sheriff suggested that Jack and the other boys leave town. Another account suggests that Jack decided on his own to leave home, to avoid possible arrest. Still another scenario indicates that Jack's stepfather had relatives in Texas, and he sent Jack away to live with them.

Whatever actually happened, Jack Slade's life was undocumented for the next few years. It was not until the spring of 1847 that he showed up, back in Illinois to enlist in the army. The Mexican-American War had begun, and Slade was anxious to be a part of it.

By then, at the age of sixteen (or he may have been eighteen), he had matured physically, but was always said to be of short stature. Some said he made up for it by being strong and muscular.

Although he served in the army for a year and a half, it became apparent during this time that he loved his liquor. Also, he disliked having to take orders from his superiors and often spent time in the stockade.

Nevertheless, when the war ended in 1848 Slade was honorably discharged.

It is believed that he then headed for California, but by 1849 he had already returned to the Midwest. In Kansas City Slade found a job with the Central Overland Company freight transportation company as a teamster. He was a good fit for the rigors of driving horse-drawn wagon shipments of goods across the 600-mile prairie to Denver.

Slade distinguished himself in this new role. His soon-to-be legendary exploits of killing and gore began with warding off Indians. This was a major part of survival when crossing the Great Plains. During his first two trips, it was said that he killed "a half-dozen Indians and several horse thieves" who attacked his caravan. The story says he cut off the ears of the Indians he killed and sent them back to the Indian chief as a warning. He was also responsible for capturing and hanging two "would-be armed robbers."

Slade was hailed as a hero and was soon promoted into management positions. He stepped up the ladder of success all the way to the position of superintendent, and was responsible for overseeing 500 miles of trail from Julesburg, to the far southwestern corner of present-day Wyoming. This was the most remote area in which the company operated.

However, stories also began circulating about Slade's killings, which often seemed to be unnecessary and unprovoked. He was said to have killed one of his own drivers while in a fit of drunken derangement. He apparently goaded this friend into drawing his gun. When the man did, Slade shot him dead and was then deeply remorseful.

Another rumor suggested he had killed still another man with no reason other than cavalier disregard. Slade bet some companions that he could shoot the button on the man's shirt from some distance away. When he accurately shot the button, he also killed the man.

The law of the Colorado West was erratic, and the number of lawmen available—especially in such isolated areas—was minimal or nonexistent.

Slade was not arrested or prosecuted for his acts. Few witnesses were willing to testify against him. Many feared him.

When Jack Slade became superintendent, he met the stationmaster of the Julesburg Station, a man named Jules Beni (sometimes spelled Reni). The settlement that had sprung up around the station was named for Beni, and he ran the place as if he owned it, causing Slade to dislike him immediately. However, at the time, Indians were Slade's bigger concern, so nothing immediately came of this personality conflict.

Around 1857 Slade met a woman named Maria Virginia. He may have met this woman he called Virginia in a dance hall, or she could have been a local widow. Whatever the case, he fell deeply in love with her and they would stay together the rest of his life. Virginia Slade said they were married, although no marriage record has ever been found.

Later that year, the Central Overland Company was having serious trouble with robberies around Julesburg. Horses and supplies were being stolen and the newly added California and Pikes Peak Express Company was also being targeted. The robbers seemed to know when wealthy passengers were aboard. Covert information suggested it was an inside job and the most likely suspect was Jules Beni.

The Company asked Jack Slade to look into the situation. Jules Beni heard rumors almost immediately about why the superintendent had come to "his" town. Slade apparently was asking questions of local citizens and indiscriminately mentioning the stationmaster in connection with the robberies. Beni did not hesitate to react, and took his shotgun with him when he went to look for Slade.

Slade was leaving a local saloon when Jules Beni walked up in front of him. Not a word was said as Beni aimed his shotgun point-blank at Slade and fired with both barrels. Slade was stunned and then fell to the ground with wounds in his chest and stomach. Beni deliberately took his time reloading his gun while the local citizens scattered to hide. He again took aim at Slade and fired two more times, hitting him in the back. Slade did not move. Beni reloaded again and shot Jack Slade one more time. Convinced he'd killed his enemy, Beni spat in the dirt and said, "Bury him!"

Slade, apparently a dead man, slowly lifted his head and said in a low voice, "I shall live long enough to wear one of your ears on my watch guard. You needn't trouble yourself about my burial."

Beni was surprised that Slade was still alive, but even more surprised that the outraged citizens of "his" town pulled their guns on him and arrested him. In a quick decision, the crowd decided to lynch Beni on the spot.

Although a correct hanging knot is designed to snap the neck of the victim as he falls from a platform, this hastily tied knot didn't work that way. Strung up and hanging, the rope tight around his neck, Beni began to suffocate. He turned blue and then almost black. Suddenly he found himself dropped to the ground as his hanging rope was released. Beni gasped and choked and lay there wheezing. An official of the freight company had just arrived on the stagecoach and fired shots in the air, demanding that the lynch mob let Beni loose.

The official was Benjamin Ficklin, General Superintendent of the Central Overland California and Pikes Peak Express Company, and he threatened Beni while the scoundrel still lay on the ground. He said Beni could live only if he promised to leave the territory and never return. Beni readily agreed. He hastily ran for his horse and rode out of town.

Slade, meanwhile, was hauled over to the station where a doctor was summoned to examine him. The doctor didn't hold out much hope for Jack Slade but worked to remove seven pellets of the dozens in his body, which came from the numerous pellets in each shotgun blast. When Slade continued to live through the night and all the next day, Ficklin ordered that the patient be transported Omaha for better medical attention. Slade painfully endured the bumpy journey that, for lack of capable doctors, ultimately proceeded on to Kansas City and finally to St. Louis.

Slade had traveled 800 miles, and though wounded and very weak, he hung onto life. His injuries were so severe that he would be hospitalized for a full year. When he was finally released, the "prescription" given to him by his doctors was to retire.

Nine days later Jack Slade was back at work for his former company and was headed for Julesburg. His mission was to kill Jules Beni, just as he had sworn to do a year earlier.

Beni had never left the area, despite his promise to do so, and the Company believed he was still robbing them. Slade was taking no chances this time and he sent four men ahead with a bounty to capture Beni alive. They soon found Beni and held him for Slade, who arrived shortly thereafter.

Here the story has many versions, and it is impossible to know which is true. Beni may have been tied up to a post behind a stage relay station or at his own ranch. Some stories say Slade took his time and killed Beni one bullet at a time; other accounts say it happened quickly with Slade firing two bullets into Beni's head. The certainty is that Jules Beni died that day at the hand of Jack Slade. Beni's criminal reputation was so widely known that both the military at Ft. Laramie and the stage company were glad Slade had taken care of the problem.

An additional part of the story, which is consistent in all the versions, tells that Slade cut off both of Beni's ears after he killed him. This is what Slade had promised when Beni shot him and left him to die over a year earlier. Now Slade made good on that oath. Many stories abound about how Slade carried the ears in his pocket for a long time afterward. Some say he actually did use one ear for his watch guard. He liked to display them often.

Slade remained as superintendent for the Company and did a good job for them. Reports say that he made sure the mail got out on time and that all his operations were always on schedule. Slade hired drivers and security men and stationmasters.

One applicant Slade hired was a young boy named William Cody, called Billy. In 1860 Billy was only fourteen years old, but he convinced Slade that he was a capable wagon-team driver and horseback rider. Slade's company had just embarked on a new venture called the Pony Express and he hired young Billy, who remained an employee for about two years. Many years later Billy would be called by a new and more famous name: "Buffalo Bill."

But Jack Slade couldn't keep himself out of trouble when he was drunk, and this happened more and more frequently. Stories abound about his drunken rampages, during which he freely destroyed property and often shot men without reason. Slade's wife increasingly had trouble with him too, and she tried her best to keep liquor away from him.

Sometime around 1860 is when Mark Twain traveled through Colorado and met Jack Slade. Twain, at that point of his early life, was not well known as an author. Slade likely never knew he had met the later-famous writer. But Mark Twain was very aware that he had met Jack Slade!

Twain wrote two chapters about Slade in his book, *Roughing It*. The rest of the story about Twain's breakfast with Slade at the stage stop is completed in his book this way:

> The coffee ran out. At least it was reduced to one tin-cupful, and Slade was about to take it when he saw that my cup was empty. He politely offered to fill it, but although I wanted it, I politely declined. I was afraid he had not killed anybody that morning, and might be needing diversion. But still with firm politeness he insisted on filling my cup, and said I had traveled all night and better deserved it than he—and while he talked he placidly poured the fluid, to the last drop. I thanked him and drank it, but it gave me no comfort, for I could not feel sure that he would not be sorry, presently, that he had given it away, and proceed to kill me to distract his thoughts from the loss. But nothing of the kind occurred. We left him with only twenty-six dead people to account for, and I felt a tranquil satisfaction in the thought

that in so judiciously taking care of No. 1 at that breakfast-table I had pleasantly escaped being No. 27. Slade came out to the coach and saw us off, first ordering certain rearrangements of the mail-bags for our comfort, and then we took leave of him, satisfied that we should hear of him again, some day, and wondering in what connection.

Indeed, Mark Twain would hear about Jack Slade again.

The Central Overland California and Pikes Peak Express Company finally decided to transfer Slade to a new station along a new run, and Slade picked out the site himself. It was a beautiful valley northwest of present-day Ft. Collins, Colorado. Still endeared to his loyal wife, he decided to name the station for her. He called it Virginia Dale.

Slade's problem with drinking didn't improve in the new location. Reports from all around the region revealed Slade's continued drunken bouts and questionable gun battles, brawls, and killings that seemed to have no provocation. By now, U.S. Marshals from Denver were threatening the Central Overland California and Pikes Peak Express Company with criminal responsibility for their employee's actions.

The Company fired Jack Slade in 1862. He and his wife Virginia left the Virginia Dale Station peacefully and moved to Virginia City, in present-day Montana, where Slade started up a freight company. The venture was short lived, and, it turned out, so was Slade. In 1864, on another of his drunken rampages through the town, a local vigilante group captured and lynched him. Mark Twain heard of Jack Slade's demise, and devoted the second of the two "Slade chapters" in the book *Roughing It* reporting the details of this lynching.

Jack Slade died with a legacy of having been a good man to some and a bad man to others. Buffalo Bill Cody would later write: "Slade, although rough at times and always a dangerous character—having killed many a man—was always kind to me. During the two years that I worked for him as pony express-rider and stage-driver, he never spoke an angry word to me."

James Gordon, Murderer

J ames Gordon feared for his life as the mob outside his jail cell shouted, "Hang him! Hang him!" The mayor stood on the balcony above pleading with the crowd to desist and allow the law to take its course. He could see that his words were useless in quelling the masses. They would not be denied. James Gordon was alive for the moment, but wouldn't be for much longer.

Young James Gordon was only twenty-three years old when he arrived on the banks of Cherry Creek in Denver in 1860. Denver was such a small "spot in the road" that it was hardly recognized as a town. Like neighboring Auraria it was little more than a collection of shacks and tents. Yet both towns were already vying for status as "the best city," despite the fact that there was not one glass window to be seen in either place. The population numbered in the low thousands. Rugged flat streets of hard natural clay weren't very forgiving to the legs of horses or stiff wagon wheels. The Platte River and Cherry Creek ran so low most of the time that early explorers had called this land "uninhabitable" for its lack of water. When the waterways weren't running low, they were flooding after a ten-minute cloudburst. It was one extreme or the other.

The spectacularly beautiful panorama of the Rocky Mountains provided the backdrop for these struggling cities on the plains. Jagged 14,000-foot peaks ran from Longs Peak on the north to Pikes Peak on the south, and were arrayed with snow and glaciers year-round. Looking up

This "Hanging Tree" along Cherry Creek has remnants of ropes from past lynch-ings visible on the lower limb.
CO Historical Society, F20859

into this vista from the tawdry downtown streets only served to remind the plainsmen that life here was always lived at the extremes.

The new attraction to this rough place was gold in the nearby hills. Silver was also found in plentiful amounts. The California Gold Rush of 1849 had passed right by Denver but was now moving in reverse. Within ten years, the miners who had played out their stakes in California came back to Colorado to take advantage of its new ore discoveries. New immigrants also came from the Midwest and the East. They were all called '59ers. More extremes came in the form of "boom or bust" depending on how well the mines produced.

James Gordon should have been a gentleman. He was considered pleasant and likable and he made friends easily. He stood 6 feet tall and was physically well built. His hair was light and wavy, his eyes were blue, his complexion was clear, and he had a charming smile. These endowments alone made the man a rarity in the raw West, but he possessed yet another amazing feature for the time; he was well educated, as an engineer. He'd also had a decent upbringing by his father, a farmer.

However, even before James and his father had settled on a new farm a few miles north of Denver, young Gordon already had a tarnished reputation. It was said that he had knifed a man in Iowa, and that the root of his problem was his hellacious nature when drunk. He drank hard and became mean and reckless.

His father's farm held no interest for James. He liked excitement, and lawless Denver held every kind of corrupting adventure that might interest and entertain a young man. There were plenty of drinking establishments, gambling dens, and bordellos. It didn't take long for James Gordon to gravitate to the lowest level of scalawags and scoundrels. It was easy to slip into a wild and ruthless lifestyle in such a place.

Every western town eventually had to wage the fight that pitted decency against crime. Now it was Denver's turn to wage the battle, and so far it hadn't been winning. James Gordon was about to challenge almost everyone in Denver. Even some of the town's worst would be shocked by his actions.

It began on Wednesday, July 18, 1860. Young James started drinking in a saloon on Arapahoe Street. The more he drank, the meaner he became. He was soon drawing his pistol and waving it in the air. His behavior was understandably making patrons uncomfortable and the bartender, Frank O'Neill, protested. Gordon aimed his gun at O'Neill and, without warning, shot the bartender down.

The next day, James Gordon felt remorse. He went to visit the recovering victim, who had somehow managed to survive. He apologized and seemed to have truly regretted his actions, even offering to pay the man's expenses.

On Friday, though, the "other side" of James Gordon showed up once again. This time he was with a couple of companions, wandering from saloon to saloon, drinking at each and getting drunk. He visited a bar called Denver Hall and then dropped into the Elephant Corral, where he met "Big Phil" and they got into a quarrel. Gordon drew his gun and shot at the man twice. He missed both times and Big Phil was smart enough to run out the back door.

Gordon moved on to the Louisiana Saloon on Blake Street, shooting at a dog along the way. Angered when the bartender brought him whiskey, but no water, he threw the bottle against the wall behind the bar, where it destroyed several more bottles. Many alarmed patrons headed for the door, but Gordon stood in the way of one German man named Jacob Gantz, who had come to Denver from Leavenworth in Kansas Territory.

Gordon lost his senses completely when Gantz refused his offer of some whiskey. The German ran out the door with Gordon in hot pursuit. When Gordon caught up with him, he threatened Gantz by holding him down and pointing his gun at the terrified man's head. Gordon then cocked his gun and pulled the trigger, but no bullet fired. Again and again, the gun was cocked and the trigger was pulled, without result. Gantz begged for his life each time. At the last pull, a bullet finally discharged. Gantz was dead instantly, and Gordon stood up to celebrate.

Those who watched the tragedy unfold ran for their own safety. This gave Gordon a chance to stumble off down a side street, where he passed out in some bushes and slept through the entire night. When he woke up, he was surprised to learn from another drunk that a mob was searching for him, ready to lynch him on the spot.

Gordon fled on a horse toward Fort Lupton, north of Denver. He was pursued by the mob-turned-vigilantes, who soon had him surrounded. But Gordon was able to elude them and sneaked off into the brush along the Platte River. His pursuers returned to Denver empty-handed. In the meantime, Gordon procured a mule and, avoiding the main roads, traveled more than 200 miles south across the eastern plains to Bent's Fort.

Back in Denver, a bounty had been raised to capture Gordon. A man named W.H. Middaugh was appointed to go after him. He hunted along the Platte River for ten days without success and believed that James Gordon's trail had gone dry. As it turned out, Gordon himself would lead Middaugh in the right direction.

James Gordon decided to write a letter to one of his friends in Denver. He entrusted it to a man headed north from Bent's Fort, who planned to pass through Denver. The man promised to deliver it. Meanwhile, Middaugh and a deputy were tracking south of Denver trying to pick up some sign of Gordon. Purely by accident, they came across the man carrying Gordon's letter. When Middaugh described what Gordon looked like, the man said he had just seen him at Bent's Fort. He turned the letter over to Middaugh and told him that Gordon was leaving the fort for Texas on a forty-team wagon convoy.

By the time the Middaugh team reached the convoy, they discovered that Gordon had already left the wagon train and was headed first for Fort Gibson and then south through Indian Territory through present-day Oklahoma. James had joined with four other men to assure safe passage through Indian country. Middaugh forged ahead and continued in dogged pursuit of Gordon.

At a small town along the route, Middaugh learned that Gordon was just a day ahead. The sheriff of Coffey County, Kansas Territory joined Middaugh and his deputy. They picked up fresh horses and kept up a fast pace. Within a day, they came across a farmer who thought he'd seen the man they were seeking at a nearby village. When they reached this place, local inhabitants said Gordon had left only half an hour earlier.

James Gordon felt sure that he had eluded his pursuers long ago. He had no reason to suspect anyone was looking for him now. Confidently and casually, he stopped along the road and let his mule graze in a small meadow. He was totally unnerved when Middaugh and his group rode up and drew their guns on him. They disarmed him of his Colt .44-caliber revolver and his derringer, and then arrested him.

At the closest blacksmith shop, double irons were fashioned to manacle Gordon. Rather than travel through the isolated and remote plains back to Denver, Middaugh chose to take Gordon to nearby Leavenworth, in Kansas Territory, where they could meet up with a stage line. Middaugh had not, however, figured on the reception they would receive there.

Jacob Gantz, the man murdered by Gordon, was originally from Leavenworth. He had been well known in the large German community, and when locals heard that Gantz's killer had been captured, a lynch mob formed. The courthouse was surrounded and chants of "Hang him! Hang him!" rang out from the crowd. Mayor McDowell attempted to calm the mob, but it was to no avail. Throughout the night bonfires illuminated the waiting mob, which continued to grow. Peddlers circulated through the crowd hawking food to those who had missed dinner in order to stand sentinel at the courthouse.

Legal wrangling ensued over who maintained official jurisdiction of Gordon. A disputed decision by the presiding judge ruled at first that Gordon should be set free. It was ultimately decided that Gordon needed to be protected while the legal details were being sorted out. That determination, coupled with a fear that the jailhouse might come under attack, led to an attempt to move Gordon out of the jail and into other quarters. The sheriff's posse tried to protect Gordon as they led him toward the Planters House Hotel, but the crowd soon surrounded them and placed a noose around Gordon's neck. He was pushed, battered, and bruised, and was so terrified that he begged to be shot dead right there. The posse soon regained control of Gordon with the assistance of a group of soldiers, who had been ordered in to help. The rope was cut from Gordon's neck and he was saved from certain death.

Another hearing took place and the local authorities refused to give Gordon over to Middaugh for a trip back to Denver. The officials said they needed evidence of Gordon's guilt, but would hold him until it was provided. Middaugh could do nothing but return to Denver without his prisoner.

Citizens of Denver had been apprised of Middaugh's unrelenting attempts to bring Gordon to justice, and when Middaugh returned and stepped off the stage he received a hero's welcome for his efforts in capturing Gordon. Enough money was raised to return three witnesses of Gantz's murder to Leavenworth. Middaugh accompanied them on the reverse run of the "Leavenworth to Pikes Peak" stage.

With the required proof, Gordon was finally released to the custody of Middaugh for his return to Denver. A chain was fastened around both their waists connecting them together for the long stagecoach ride.

Early in the morning on September 28, 1860, the stage from Leavenworth pulled into Denver. James Gordon was jailed to await his trial. Middaugh had covered 3,000 miles during the two months it had taken him to apprehend Gordon.

The trial began the next day. It was held by citizens in a "peoples' court" since there was no official judicial system yet established. Every effort was made to provide a fair hearing of the facts. A.C. Hunt was appointed judge; he would later become a territorial governor of Colorado. James Gordon was represented by a defense attorney. A jury was appointed. Over 1,000 people attended the trial, which took place in a grove of cottonwood trees near Wazee Street.

The trial lasted four days. Although the participants had no legal training, they were all considered to be of high character. The prosecution and defense examined and cross-examined their witnesses. The defendant was said to have been irresponsible for murder due to his condition of drunkenness. The prosecution did not accept drunkenness as an excuse, and held that he was responsible for the crime.

By October 2, the trial ended. The jury pronounced James Gordon guilty of "willful murder." Judge Hunt sentenced him to be hanged on Saturday, October 6, and young Gordon responded by bowing to the crowd.

The lawless residents of the rough town of Denver were opposed to these proceedings, since they represented a new attitude meant to undermine their power. They threatened to storm the building where Gordon was being held. The decent citizens, however, provided a guard that deterred this possibility.

On Saturday, a well-guarded buggy brought James Gordon to the scaffold that had been erected on the east bank of Cherry Creek. Middaugh had been placed in charge of the hanging at the request of young Gordon. While imprisoned, he had told guards that Middaugh had saved his life at Leavenworth. He said that hanging could not be "one-tenth as dreadful as what he had been through there," and that he had already "died a thousand deaths," only to be "saved and dragged back to the scaffold."

Thousands were present for the hanging. Members of the crowd removed their hats for a prayer while Gordon knelt. And then James Gordon was hanged less than a year after he had arrived.

Crime did not abruptly stop in Denver or Auraria due to the capture and "people's court" trial of James Gordon. Other criminals would be arrested and convicted by the same court until official law was eventually established. A new territorial government matured into statehood for Colorado.

Hoodlums were not free to run amuck as they once did. They had to consider their chances of being captured and imprisoned for their reckless acts. The young ones, especially, would have to think about whether they wanted to live beyond the age of twenty-three.

The Espinosa Gang, Terrorists

In the spring of 1863 the entire region of the country between Pueblo and Park Counties, in fact all sections of the Territory, became panic stricken by accounts of terrible and mysterious massacres of travelers on the lonely roads leading from the southwest to South Park. Every so often residents of certain localities disappeared. Later, their bodies were found. No one knew who was responsible since there were no clues." This is how the situation was so aptly described by authors George G. Everett and Wendell F. Hutchinson in their book, *Under the Angel of Shavano.* Fear was so great across South Park not only because of the murders, but because the murderer's identity remained unknown. No one knew who might be next. There were lookouts posted everywhere, but for whom? A band of Indians? A gang? Convicts on the run? A miner gone berserk?

Finally, when a lumber wagon was attacked along a road going into Fairplay, the driver saw the outlaws. One of them stood up next to the road, aimed his gun, and fired point-blank at the driver. Luckily, the bullet lodged into a copy of Lincoln's *Emancipation Proclamation,* which he was carrying in his breast pocket. Another outlaw was barely hidden in the bushes.

As the wagon raced down the hill into town, the driver memorized the two faces he had seen. They appeared to be Mexican, and they were apparently crack shots with their pistols. The driver knew that he would have been a dead man if the bullet's progress hadn't been stopped. The information he provided to authorities in Fairplay helped them connect the incident to earlier murders near Cañon City, in which the chief suspects were the Espinosas.

The brothers Jose Vivian Espinosa and Felipe Niero Espinosa were born in New Mexico Territory. Their family moved to the San Luis Valley in Colorado Territory and settled in the village of San Rafael along Conejos Creek. It was located about 2 miles west of the town of Conejos. They brought a large herd of sheep with them as a source of income. This area had been sparsely colonized by the Mexicans when it was under the ownership of Mexico, and it was so desolate that the population remained small. The Ute Indians also wandered this territory, but the Mexicans lived there relatively undisturbed and had done so for many years.

After the United States won the war with Mexico, the U.S. Cavalry built Fort Garland to oversee this southern outpost. Colorado had recently been established as a territory of the United States and was beginning to attract new settlers. With this influx of Anglo-American immigrants, the Mexican families began to feel that their domain was being invaded.

The Espinosa family claimed that grants were not being honored, and that Anglos were settling on their land without compensating them. They also claimed that their sheep had been run off, and that one child had been killed. This resentment became the catalyst for the two sons to begin a rampage throughout hundreds of miles of territory around their home.

The Espinosa brothers had already been suspected of delinquent activities such as horse stealing. They were next heard of when they stopped a wagon north of Santa Fe, which was hauling supplies to a store run by a priest. They tied up the driver, strapped him to the tongue of the wagon, and then stampeded the horses so that the man and the uncontrolled wagon lurched and pitched down the road. The priest happened to see the runaway wagon when he was out riding, and he

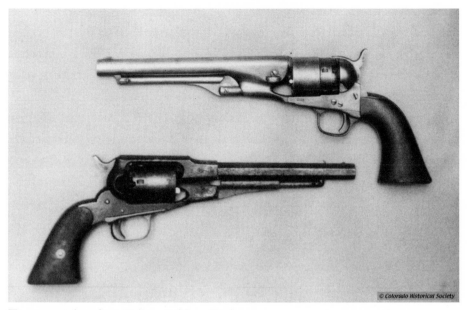

Two guns taken from Felipe and Jose Espinosa.
CO Historical Society, WPA 1183

rescued the terrified driver. The Cavalry was notified and it was determined that the Espinosas were the culprits.

Captain Eaton at Fort Garland was sent to capture the hoodlums. He led a party of fifteen soldiers, a lieutenant, a sergeant, and a deputy U.S. Marshal to San Rafael. Their plan was to act as though they were recruiting new enlistees for the U.S. Army, so the brothers would not suspect their true purpose. When they stopped to inquire at the Espinosa cabin, Jose answered the door. As a soldier talked with him, the lieutenant seized Espinosa and told him he was under arrest. Jose quickly recoiled and ducked back into the cabin, where he and Felipe drew their guns. Shooting out the door they killed one soldier as the others ran for cover. The Espinosas escaped and fled into the Sangre de Cristo Mountains. From that day in 1863 they decided it would be their mission to kill Anglos.

William Bruce lived along Hardscrabble Creek near Cañon City. He worked at a sawmill and was one day reported missing by his family, because he had not come home that afternoon. A search party went out to look for him, and they soon came across his body. He had been shot through the heart.

Sometime later, and 60 miles away in the Fountain Creek area, another man named Henry Harkens, who also worked at a sawmill, met his demise. He and some other men had built the sawmill in a small canyon, which they named Saw Mill Gulch. As the men were running the mill, Harkens worked on a cabin nearby. Late one afternoon the men came by the cabin to tell Harkens that they were headed over to look at the new road improvements in the area. Harkens stayed behind to cook dinner for the group.

The Espinosa brothers observed the men from a ridge, and waited until Harkens was alone. Then they rode down to the cabin where Harkens was cooking and shot him. The death scene was a grisly one, because the Espinosas used an axe to finish him off.

When Harkens' partners returned, they found his brutalized body next to the cabin. Inside the cabin everything had been dumped on the ground, and a suitcase and sack of flour had been slashed. Unaware of the previous killings and crimes by the Espinosas, the men believed this was an attack by Indians because of the use of what they thought was a hatchet.

Although pioneers lived primitively, the friends of Harkens made a special effort to locate a beautiful resting place for their friend's grave. When the grave was dug, they laid small logs inside it and covered them with pine boughs as a lining. Harkens' body was placed in this simple casket, covered with more limbs, and buried. The wooden marker read: "Henry Harkens, Murdered Wednesday evening, March 19th, 1863." From that time forward, the canyon was known as Dead Man's Canyon.

A sheriff and his deputy had been following the murderers from the location near Cañon City where William Bruce had been killed. They were not sure of the identity of the killers, but they soon came to the sight of Harkens' cabin where they met the funeral party. From there, the murderers had run away to Colorado City, and on to Manitou Springs. They disappeared over Ute Pass.

The sheriff and deputy pursued them all the way to the vast broad valley called South Park. There, the body of J. D. Addleman was found on his ranch where the Espinosas had killed him. At this point, the murderers were able to hide. The sheriff and his party lost their tracks and had to give up the search and go home.

Two days later, four men were found dead near South Park at Red Hill. Also killed near Red Hill were two California Gulch inhabitants named Lehman and Seyga. Bill Carter, a prospector, was robbed of his gun, money, and clothing at his claim at Cottage Grove Alma, in South Park Valley. He was then killed.

The Espinosas were so violent and savage that they were considered to be the most notorious of all Colorado outlaws. Residents in the area still did not yet know their names, but fear pervaded the community and many were afraid to be out alone or along the roads at night. All strangers were suspected. One man escaped a posse near Red Hill and was forced to flee to Fairplay, where a Methodist pastor verified his identity as a local man.

Another tragedy occurred as a result of the widespread fear surrounding the Espinosa rampage. A man named Baxter was under suspicion, perhaps because he was staying with a family where he had not been seen before. It was thought that they were hiding him. Panic and the need to take action to rid the area of the horrible murderers led a mob to surround the home and demand the man's surrender. He was taken to Fairplay and hung without a trial. It was only realized later, when the murders continued, that Baxter was innocent.

The connection was finally made between the South Park attacks and the Espinosa brothers after a wagon driver, mentioned at the beginning of the story, identified his attackers. Now it was clear who they were looking for.

Captain John McCannon led a posse to search the huge South Park region. The posse had to be divided so that they could cover the widespread parameters of the big valley. The trail of the Espinosas was eventually found, and McCannon circled his men into a large loop around their camp. They quietly moved in on Jose and Felipe as the two were tending to their horses. A posse member fired. Felipe Espinosa heard the sound of the gun and almost simultaneously was struck by a bullet that broke his second rib. A shotgun was fired which grazed the horses, and another shot struck Felipe between his eyes. Felipe was killed, but

This old law enforcement postcard represents a threat like that of the Espinosas.
CO Historical Society

Jose scrambled away and fled. The posse had difficulty distinguishing young Espinosa from their own men, and lost him when he crossed a nearby ravine. A book, which was found on the body of Felipe Espinosa, stated that twenty-two Americans had been killed by the duo.

Jose traveled all the way back south to the family home in the San Luis Valley. Along the way, he is reported to have killed two more men near Cañon City and another in Conejos. When he arrived in San Rafael he told the family of Felipe's death. A young twelve-year-old nephew then joined Jose to ride out and continue the rampage.

The Espinosas heard news that the territorial governor of Colorado, John Evans, was visiting in the San Luis Valley. Evans was on government business at Conejos, meeting with the Utes regarding new land boundaries. Stories suggest that the Espinosas were near Evans' camp and either did not recognize him, in order to assassinate him, or decided on another plan. In a letter written to the territorial governor, the Espinosas threatened that the killing would continue unless the governor compensated them for the family's stolen land. This may have led to the governor's offer of a reward of $1,500 (some say it was $2,500) for the capture of the Espinosas, dead or alive. Some accounts of this story say that Governor Evans never offered a reward.

Jose Espinosa and his nephew stayed in seclusion for a brief period, but came out of hiding near Fort Garland. Nearby, a buggy carrying an American man and his Mexican wife was traveling along the road. The couple was on their way to Costilla, New Mexico Territory from Trinidad, Colorado Territory by way of a canyon in the Sangre de Cristo Mountains. The Espinosas encountered them, and seeing the American man shot at them killing one of the mules pulling the buggy. The man jumped from the buggy and ran up the hill. As the Espinosas were chasing the man up the hillside, the woman hid. Two Mexicans happened to be riding along in their wagon when they saw her. One of the men was named Pedro Garcia. He told the woman to get into his wagon and she told Garcia and his friend what had been happening. When the Espinosas quit chasing the man, they returned to the road and realized the woman was gone. They saw the men in the wagon trying to escape with the woman, but the Espinosas were able to stop them. The Espinosas took her as a hostage, and told Garcia to drive away. One of the desperadoes announced that they were "the Espinosas."

In the meantime, the man who had successfully escaped the Espinosas headed for Fort Garland. When he reached it, he reported the hold-up to the commanding officer, Colonel Sam Tappan, who sent sol-diers in search of the woman who had been kidnapped. They found Pedro Garcia along the way, and he informed them that the kidnappers were the murderous Espinosas. The soldiers found the woman, who had been tied up and assaulted. She was returned to Fort Garland and was reunited with her husband. The Espinosas, however, were nowhere to be seen.

Colonel Tappan knew all about the Espinosas' murder spree and was determined to put an end to their madness. He knew of a scout named Tom Tobin, who lived nearby on Trinchera Creek. In the summer, Tobin raised cattle on his ranch where he lived with his Mexican wife and small daughter. They lived in Costilla the rest of the year. Tom was illiterate and, perhaps because of that, was a strong backer of the local school. He even served as the president of the school board at one time.

Tom also had been a mountain man and an excellent scout for the military. He had a reputation for being able to track down anything. The thirty-eight year old Tobin rode a black horse, and wore a black hat and black clothing along with a pair of revolvers on his belt. Colonel Tappan asked him to find the Espinosas and bring him their heads. Tobin was interested in ending the tirade of course, but he was also interested in the reward everyone said had been offered. Tobin usually worked alone, but Tappan provided troops to accompany him since the Espinosas were believed to still be in the area.

Almost immediately Tobin found the Espinosas' tracks. He chased them through a forest, lost them, and picked up their tracks again near a streambed. Tobin could see them in the distance, but lost them again as they galloped over a ridge.

Tobin and the soldiers camped in the mountains. Then he took just a few of the men with him to search along La Veta Creek. They found oxen tracks, and Tobin was sure the Espinosas had stolen the animals for butchering. Jose and his nephew would need to eat, and Tobin thought the Espinosas were likely to be low on provisions. Tobin followed on foot until he came upon the camp.

In a surprise ambush, Tobin rushed into the camp with his muzzle-loading rifle. Jose grabbed his gun, but was struck down by a bullet from Tobin's rifle before he could shoot. He yelled to his nephew to run and escape.

The boy ran and Tobin called for his soldiers to fire upon him, but every round missed. Tobin reloaded his rifle and took aim at the boy, who was still running. When he fired, the bullet hit the boy and he was killed.

Jose was still alive and had crawled for cover. He raised his revolver and aimed at Tobin, who ducked to the side. The bullet missed Tobin and another nearby soldier. Tobin returned gunfire and killed Jose. Responding to the request by Colonel Tappan, Tobin brought back the heads of Jose Espinosa and his nephew in a gunnysack. The Espinosas had been on a rampage for several months, and Thomas Tate Tobin had captured and killed them in just three days.

Tom Tobin's story of how he killed the Espinosas made him a legend. He was never paid a reward, which some reports said Governor Evans had never actually offered. Other accounts indicate Tobin did receive a $1,500 reward, but it took him years to collect. And still another version of the story tells of Tobin receiving a silver inlaid rifle. Colonel George L. Shoup gave him $200, because his brother had been one of the men killed by the Espinosas. Tobin eventually moved permanently to the Trinchera ranch in 1872 and remained there the rest of his life. His daughter, Pasquala, married a local boy, the son of Kit Carson.

The remaining members of the Espinosa family and the other Mexican families of southern Colorado Territory eventually resolved the legal complications regarding land grants in the area. Not all were pleased with the court rulings that limited some of the territory their families claimed. The only thing they knew would be certain, and uncontestable, was that the new immigrants would keep coming.

Jim Reynolds, Confederate Guerilla

Vernon Crow was looking for buried treasure. He had heard all of the stories about the Reynolds Gang, and the riches they had left behind in the Colorado mountains. It had to be someplace nearby, he thought. He had already found the rusted knife with its handle broken off. It had been lodged in a tree at his ranch on Handcart Creek, not 50 miles from Denver. The knife was said to point to a gang member's grave.

Crow soon found the grave with a man's skeletal remains inside. The man had been buried with his boots on and there was a bullet hole in his skull. Another version of this story suggests that there was no skull, only the skeleton. Not far away, Crow found remnants of a roughly built corral and a possible lookout point behind a wall of stacked rocks. He was sure he had found the old Reynolds camp. Although further searching revealed nothing more, he thought that there was treasure out there somewhere.

Vernon Crow knew that legends had estimated Reynolds' stolen treasure to be between $3,000 and $100,000 in gold, paper money, diamonds, and jewelry. None of it had ever been recovered from those in the gang who had been arrested or killed. And there was no evidence that those who escaped had taken it with them.

Crow later told people about finding the camp, which brought legions of other fortune hunters to the area. They, and myriad more treasure seekers through the years, have never given up the search. Treasure, it's believed, is buried out there somewhere.

The Reynolds Gang's escapades were so brief and insignificant that it is surprising their story is still of interest to latter-day Coloradans.

Perhaps the story's popularity has less to do with the gang's adventures and more to do with the large booty rumored to be left behind. There is something enticing and irresistible about the promise of buried treasure.

Young Jim Reynolds was born in Texas, probably in the early 1840s. He first showed up in the annals of Colorado history in 1863. South Park is the sprawling and beautiful open valley surrounding Fairplay where Reynolds and his cronies tried to find work that interested them. They tried mining in the mountains that circled the valley, but always seemed to be moving on to the next mining settlement. They could not find, nor hold down, a good job. Maybe it was because hard work was not suited to them, or because their drinking and brawling did not lend itself well to completing a full day's work. The money they did earn went toward good horses and liquor.

Although they finally gave up their jobs entirely, they continued to have plenty of money to spend. This did not go unnoticed in the community. Several thefts of nominal amounts of money were occurring and Reynolds and his buddies were suspected. Stages were being held up and the passengers robbed. Stage stations kept only small amounts of money on hand, but robbers were stealing from them too.

Eventually, a larger robbery was attempted when the Spotswood and McClelland coach was held up. This time, a posse had been gathered to ward off the robbers. They caught the thieves in the act, but the hoodlums scattered. Jim Reynolds, however, was arrested and taken to jail in Denver. Jailhouses of that era were log shacks at best, and it wasn't long before Jim and a couple of his cellmates managed to escape. They all fled Denver.

Reynolds turned up back in Texas at the height of the Civil War. Instead of joining the army, Jim thought he could help out the South in a better way. One of the primary needs of the Confederacy was money. Their funds were being depleted at an alarming rate. When Reynolds heard this, he took it upon himself to organize his own guerrilla unit. His plan was to steal Colorado gold and silver, with the intention of bringing it back to the South to fund the war. He found twenty-three men to join him, including his younger brother, John Reynolds.

In the spring of 1864, Reynolds led his group out of Texas toward Colorado Territory. Although he said he had been commissioned by the Texas Confederate Forces, a record of this appointment has never been found. He was apparently devoted to his quest though, because all of his guerrilla volunteers were required to take an oath of allegiance to the cause.

While passing through New Mexico Territory on their way to Colorado Territory, the group happened upon a wagon train. It was too tempting a target to pass up and when they robbed it, $60,000 was turned over to them. The gang disappeared into the Spanish Peaks and bided their time until the ensuing search for them had finally been abandoned. The men, with nothing on their minds except the thought of all that money, began to instigate an uprising against Reynolds. He maintained that the minted coins that they had stolen were to be used for the Confederacy, as the men had declared in their oaths. Conveniently forgetting the oath, however, most of the men wanted their share of the loot then and there.

Reynolds had no choice but to pay them, although he demanded they leave his gang. Most of his guerrillas took their money and rode away. Only nine traveled on to Colorado Territory: Jim, his brother John, Owen Singleterry, Jake Stowe, Tom Holliman, John Bobbitt, John Andrews, Jack Robinson, and Tom Knight.

The group scattered to avoid attention and reassembled at the designated site of Adolph Guirand's ranch between Hartsel and Fairplay. Jim Reynolds knew Guirand and his wife from his earlier days in Colorado Territory. Although the Guirands may not have expected or desired their new guests, the gang was fed and sheltered there.

As the gang moved on toward Fairplay, they began their pillage on behalf of the South. It started out with small encounters. They came across the superintendent of the Phillips Lode and robbed him. His name was Major H. H. deMary, and Reynolds had heard stories of the

Fairplay, Colorado in 1860.
Denver Public Library, Western History Collection, X-8331

gold he kept in buckets and jars. Unfortunately, deMary was only carrying a few dollars with him that day. This must have upset Reynolds, because he decided to take deMary with them as a prisoner. They forced deMary to exchange hats with one of the gang members, but the hat was too small. One of the gang forced it down over deMary's ears and made fun of him.

As they headed for McLaughlin's stage station, a few more robberies along the way also yielded little. But Reynolds had been tipped off that the McLaughlin stage was carrying a rich shipment and that was his main target.

At McLaughlin's, 10 miles out of Fairplay, the gang rode in and immediately took over the station. They disarmed the people there and Reynolds ordered the cook to fix them dinner. The gang wined and dined with much amusement.

When the stage arrived, the only passenger was the owner of the line. He was robbed of about $400 and his gold watch. The driver was ordered to hand over the mail, and the strongbox was forced open with an axe. Figures from $3,000 to $100,000 were given as the total amount stolen in currency, gold, and jewelry. The guerillas also stole the horses and, before riding off, chopped the spokes out of the wheels of the stage. They then freed Major deMary.

Mail was of extreme importance to people in the frontier towns and mining camps. It was the only way to stay in contact with relatives in distant places, and for some it was the lifeline for transferring money back home. A Fairplay prostitute had mailed $200 to her sick mother in Springfield, Illinois. When she heard the stage had been robbed, she was bereft and angry. Others had also lost important documents and funds.

Although the alert had gone out to many local communities after this robbery, the Reynolds Gang had moved on with little haste. At a place called Michigan House they stole more horses. When they reached Kenosha Pass they stopped in for a meal at the Kenosha House. Then they continued on and stayed overnight at the Omaha House, a two-story building where the gang decided to remain and relax for a while.

A lone man, named Mr. Berry, had been tracking the gang ever since the incident at the McLaughlin stage station. He was from the nearby town of Hamilton where he had first ridden to warn the community about the outlaws. Berry rode on to Kenosha Pass and found a man named Hall to accompany him. They arrived at Omaha House, but were captured by Reynolds. Berry's and Hall's pistols were taken from them, as well as Hall's necktie pin.

The gang was in good spirits and talked easily with Berry and Hall. They told them they had come to Colorado Territory to steal gold, silver, and treasure, and return with it to give to the Confederacy. One of the gang pulled pieces of the stolen stage mail from his pocket and joked about it. Finally they released the two men and even returned Hall's necktie pin to him when they learned it had been given to him by a friend. Berry and Hall left Omaha House and rode to Junction House, located at the junction of the road to Evergreen and the road to Denver, to warn residents there. Berry then continued on to Denver to warn more people of the guerrillas.

Reynolds and his gang were still unaware of any potential trouble, so they rode out and hid outside Junction House. Although the residents had been warned, Reynolds' gang was able to quietly steal more horses there without being seen. Then they returned to Omaha House for another night.

Their peaceful traveling was soon to end, however, as several posses were now headed their way. Captain Maynard had set out from Denver with his posse, as had Marshal Dave Cook and his group. Jack Sparks, from Swan River—near Breckenridge—led a posse from the north. And Major deMary, who had earlier suffered ridicule at the hands of the gang, had formed a posse of thirty men coming from Fairplay.

Reynolds was very familiar with this territory, and as they headed up to Shaffer's Crossing he could see deMary's posse down below. He decided to lead his band off the main road and onto a mountain trail up Handcart Gulch. Here the gang hurriedly built a makeshift camp and a corral for their horses. Rocks were built up as protection so a lookout could be posted to watch the valley below.

The Reynolds Gang would have to hide out there until they could make their next move. While they waited and watched, they had an opportunity to bury their treasure. Since stealing it at the stage station out of Fairplay, they would have had to transport it along with them on their journey. It was probably somewhat cumbersome, but they had no real need to unload it until they were pressured by the posses. If they wanted to stash it so they could make a quick getaway, this would be a likely place. They could plan to come back for it later when the law was not hot on their trail.

Major deMary's posse continued along the main road passing right by the side trail where Reynolds had led his gang. Captain Maynard's posse arrived at Kenosha House to find that the gang had already left. One of Maynard's troops had trailed behind and saw the Reynolds Gang heading away, so he rode back to alert his captain. But by the time Maynard's men got the tip and turned around, they had lost the gang and Maynard ended up taking his posse back to Denver. Cook's group continued on to Fairplay, missing everyone.

Only Jack Sparks' posse was headed toward the camp where the Reynolds Gang was holed up. But it was completely by accident. Sparks and his men arrived at the top of Handcart Gulch at nightfall, and decided to set up camp there. They were not aware that the Reynolds Gang was camped close by. One of Sparks' men thought he saw a flicker of light beyond them in the woods. On foot, the posse closed in on what turned out to be a campfire. Realizing that they had stumbled onto Reynolds' hiding place, Sparks directed his men to encircle the gang's camp. Apparently one of Sparks' posse charged in too soon and accidentally alerted the Reynolds Gang, who were then able to run for cover. The two groups fired at each other through the darkness, but the gang mounted their horses and escaped.

The Sparks posse rode to Kenosha House to spend the night there. When they rode back to Reynolds' camp the next day, they found the body of Owen Singleterry. He had apparently been shot in the crossfire of the previous night and died there. Singleterry had been Reynolds' top aide. Sparks' posse buried him near the camp, and his knife was stuck in a tree trunk pointing to his grave. The Reynolds Gang had scattered in various directions to elude the posse. Tom Holliman rode to Cañon City, where he found a room and fell asleep. Some of Sparks' posse followed him there and easily surprised and captured him. Holliman was taken back to Fairplay and jailed. John Reynolds, Jake Stowe, and John Andrews were closely pursued to the south, but made it back into New Mexico Territory. It is believed that Stowe suffered wounds in the shootout in Handcart Gulch and died after the gang arrived. Andrews was said to have been killed in a saloon brawl in Texas. John Reynolds would remain at large and probably fled the territory. Jim Reynolds and three others retreated into the hills and also remained at large. None were believed to have been able to carry any treasure with them on their hasty retreat.

Two days later, Jim Reynolds and his now much smaller gang, reappeared at a ranch outside of Fairplay. Desperate for food and shelter, the men took over the ranch. Sighted by lookouts in the area, Reynolds' band was pursued and barely escaped. A new posse led by Captain Shoup was made up of seventy-five men, supply wagons, and cooks. This allowed Shoup to send out separate units to cover a wide swath of the territory.

The Reynolds Gang was unable to outmaneuver this large network. Fleeing southeast, they were finally pinned down east of Cañon City. Capture of all four men was made without resistance. They and their other partner Tom Holliman (who had been brought from Fairplay), were all taken to Denver. No portion of the stolen loot was found on the men.

Although Colorado was not officially involved in the Civil War, many residents were sympathizers of one side or the other. The friends of the Confederacy were fewer in number than the Unionists, so the arrest of the pro-southern Reynolds Gang created a stir in Denver. Local officials were concerned that some southern-leaning locals might attempt to free the five jailed men.

To avoid such a problem, the five guerrillas were turned over to the local military division for protection. Strange events followed which all took place secretly, so there are no records to verify or disclaim them. The story told is that the army held a secret trial and found all the members of the Reynolds Gang guilty of conspiring against the United States Government. They were all sentenced to hanging.

However, there was public concern that the military may have over-stepped its authority. In response to these questions, it was announced that the prisoners would be taken to Fort Leavenworth, Kansas to have their case reviewed. The 3rd Colorado Cavalry, under Captain Cree, escorted the five gang members out of Denver.

The next day, another odd occurrence baffled local citizens, when the captain and his troops returned without the prisoners. The captain said that all five men had been killed when they tried to escape. It would not be learned until a later date what had actually happened. A local scout, traveling from Fort Leavenworth, came across the old ghost town of Russellville and stopped to look around. There, he found the bodies of five men lashed to trees, all shot to death. Cree later maintained he was told to kill the men as soon as he could, and that there was never any intention to deliver them to Fort Leavenworth.

John Reynolds, Jim's brother, is said to have returned to Colorado Territory in 1871. One story says he may have looked for the buried treasure, but must have been unable to find it because he and another outlaw took up horse stealing due to lack of funds. When John was mortally wounded in one of the raids, legend says he drew a map of the treasure's location so his partner could try to find it. His partner likely did not find it either, since it was reported that he died in Wyoming, penniless.

Jim Reynolds' misadventures did not ultimately help fund the Confederacy. Apparently, no one would benefit financially from his thievery. Unless, someday, a person hiking in the mountains between Kenosha Pass and Shaffer's Crossing happens to turn up a rock and find treasure hidden beneath it.

The Musgrove Gang, Horse Thieves

The *Rocky Mountain News* reported in 1868 that "Musgrove was an outlaw who had made society his prey for several years, successively defying by boldness, when he could not outwit by cunning, the officers of justice . . . he soon became the recognized chief of a band of land pirates, who lived by running off government stock, effacing the brand and then disposing of it."

Lee Musgrove was born in Como, Mississippi probably sometime in the early 1830s. He had little education, but was said to be very bright and a natural leader. By 1849, he had grown into a tall, physically imposing young man. The California gold fields were ripe with the promise of adventure and wealth, so Musgrove decided to go there to begin his adult life. He left home and traveled to the Napa Valley, where he joined the search for gold. Soon though, he realized the odds were not in his favor for striking it rich.

As the Civil War was brewing in the East, he stayed in California and worked at temporary jobs. Being a southerner he might have gone back home and joined the Confederacy. Instead, he chose to remain in the West, but couldn't restrain himself from fighting his own "war" there. In 1861 he was involved in a heated argument, in which he sided in favor of the South's secession. The argument ended when Musgrove killed his defenseless rival.

Musgrove left the Napa Valley to avoid retaliation and headed to Nevada Territory. His defense of the South continued as a personal vendetta when he killed two more men in arguments there. He moved on to Cheyenne, Wyoming Territory, where yet another man's derision of the South inflamed him so much that he killed this adversary as well.

Musgrove had to flee again, and this time he went to Denver. By now, the Civil War was coming to an end, and Musgrove maintained a low-key lifestyle while working in the area for about a year. He ranged as far as Fort Halleck, in Wyoming Territory, which was a center for Indian trade. Musgrove was involved in business dealings there. All went peacefully for him until an Indian called him a liar, which triggered Musgrove's short temper. He calmly drew his gun and shot the Indian in the head.

On the run again, Musgrove soon disappeared into the unknown. His name would not be heard again until 1868.

Marshal Dave Cook had been installed to clean up the lawless and wild activities pervading the young city of Denver. After his arrival in 1863 as a military detective, Cook had quickly established himself as the veritable force that would wipe out crime in Denver. His success in ferreting out criminals and bringing them to justice for the U.S. Army led to his election as city marshal. Denver was able to enjoy an unusual period of peace from the hoodlums who were moving into towns all over the West.

In late 1867, the first report of a potential new threat came to Cook in a message from Kansas Territory. Thirty horses had been stolen from a rural ranch. A week later, a report from New Mexico Territory informed him of a small community where homes and stores had been burglarized and the stagecoach had been held up. Next he heard from Wyoming Territory that fifty horses had gone missing. Utah Territory reported a raid by a gang. The territories of Nebraska, Texas, and Arizona all reported that small settlements had been targeted.

The striking thing about all these reports was that the criminals and their booty all seemed to disappear into oblivion. Each crime was expertly planned and timed to maximize the greatest take. And the outlaws, as well as whole herds of horses, were not traceable.

Lee Musgrove hanged by a Denver lynch mob at the Larimer Street bridge over Cherry Creek.

From "Hands Up!" Reminiscences by D.J. Cook, University of Oklahoma Press, 1958

By early 1868, every territory bordering Colorado Territory had been hit by the raids. Finally, it would be included when forty horses were stolen from one horse breeder in the southeastern part of the territory. When these events first began, the local authorities in each location were unaware that the other crimes were occurring. They had no way of knowing of the similarities in all these offenses across the eight-territory region.

Marshal Cook, however, had organized an association of his cohorts in law enforcement during the previous few years. He had seen the need to establish better interaction among crime fighters in the region. The old method for chasing down wanted criminals was for the local sheriff to follow the clues by himself, even if they led him across several territories. Cook suggested that lawmen work together and help one another in making arrests in other jurisdictions. His group was called the Rocky Mountain Detective Association. It was through this group that one of his associates first alerted him to widespread gang activity in the other territories. Soon all of the affected territories' law officers were notified of the extent of the crimes.

It was obvious to Cook that the raids had similar planning, suggesting they were somehow connected. He suspected the gangs' activities were masterminded by an individual, someone who was capable of outsmarting him and the other law enforcement officials in several regions. The question was who? And where was this leader headquartered?

Cook reasoned that there could be only one place for the gang leader to hide himself, and it was right under his nose. It had to be Denver. It was geographically located in the center of all the raid activity. Messengers could easily ride in and out carrying instructions. It was the region's largest city, which made it easy for someone to remain concealed. And since Cook had quieted the outlaw faction, no one would suspect that any desperado would choose to live there.

By involving his extensive association in the matter, Cook began to piece the information together. Local association affiliates were asked to look for signs of stock for sale and to trace the sellers. Every detail of the raids was studied. Denver's underworld was infiltrated for clues to anyone connected to the gang. A vague trail of information gradually began to form.

These efforts finally led to one man. The prime suspect was Lee Musgrove, the notorious criminal wanted for murder in nearly every territory of the region. His partners were also revealed to be two other killers named Ed Franklin and Jack Willetson.

Musgrove had been busy since he had gone underground three years before. Being a wanted man, he had to stay concealed. For income he began stealing horses, which led to larger scale raids using recruited men. He began to plan a regional operation running up and down the Rocky Mountains. Musgrove could mastermind the operation while other outlaws would complete the missions. Estimates suggest that as many as 200 men were part of Musgrove's scheme. They included hardened horse thieves, highwaymen, and murderers. It was the largest outlaw syndicate of the Old West.

This lawless group was divided into factions throughout the Rockies and some bordering territories. Musgrove placed the outlaw gangs in mountain and plains areas. He oversaw the planning and coordinated every detail of the raids, appointing various experienced hoodlums to lead each operation. The gangs struck with precision, and always seemed to know when their victims were in the most vulnerable position. His plans always included ways to escape that would thwart pursuers.

Raids were only made out on the open prairie or at isolated locations. Rural ranches were favorite targets that allowed stolen horse herds to be driven out into the desolate countryside. By the time posses could be formed to chase them, the gangs and their stolen herds had already disappeared into hundreds of miles of backcountry. They could ride for days, unseen by another human. The horses would be moved as far as 250 to 500 miles away.

These bands had been operating, unhindered by the law, for three months. Their operations were so simple and effective that the outlaws were able to carry out the disposal of their stolen horses in the midst of the public. Once the herd arrived in a chosen town it was shipped by railroad to a more financially advantageous market. Moved rapidly and across huge distances, the horses arrived in the destination city, and local officials were completely unaware that they had been stolen. Pursuing law enforcement officials were left far behind.

It was not unusual for horses stolen in Colorado Territory to end up in Texas, while those stolen in Utah Territory might end up in Arizona Territory. The horses were then placed for public sale in the new market without arousing any suspicion.

With the horses sold, the gang was free to commit another raid near where they had sold their last herd. Musgrove had the next victim already targeted, and the outlaws moved into action again carrying out the same method of moving a stolen herd to a distant locale. This efficiency in planning resulted in a string of thefts that occurred with great regularity.

Marshal Cook was highly frustrated with his inability to locate Musgrove. If the leader could be found the rest of the scheme could be broken. Although it was certain that Musgrove and his assistants operated out of Denver, they were often out of town overseeing various raids and attending to business. Each gang leader had to turn over the profits from their thefts to Musgrove, so rendezvous points had been set up in isolated locations. Payoffs were made first to the leader, and then distributed to his men.

Cook was soon notified by one of the association members that men on horseback had been seen about 30 miles from Denver near the Elmore Ranch. The men appeared to be scouting the ranch, which fit the profile of a Musgrove raid. Marshal Cook figured this might be his opportunity to stop a raid so he left immediately for the ranch. Local guards were set up that night in case the men returned. About 2:00 A.M., four men swooped down upon the ranch and rallied its herd of horses. In the midst of this activity, the guards ran out and fired on the horse thieves, who returned gunfire and ran off, leaving the horses behind.

Marshal Cook arrived shortly after the attempted theft and pursued the outlaws into the mountains. When they circled back on their way to Denver, Cook cut them off and fired his gun at them. The men fled to a cabin, but gave up when one of them was wounded by Cook. After they were arrested, one of the arrogant outlaws said that Musgrove would come and rescue them. When Cook said he didn't think Musgrove was in town, the outlaw said Musgrove had left for a while to avoid some guy named Cook.

Because of the arrest of these four men, word was out to Musgrove that returning to Denver would be dangerous. The organization began to fold from that moment.

With Musgrove in hiding, messages to his gangs became disrupted. By now, other gangs were being traced using the information Cook had sent through the association. Six gang members were apprehended in Wyoming Territory as they tried to sell horses from Nebraska Territory. Four more were arrested in what is now Arizona. Kansas Territory citizens captured three gang members and lynched them on the spot. One of Musgrove's messengers was found at Georgetown, in Colorado Territory, and brought to Denver's jail.

Although some members of the gang were arrested, the rest of the outlaws were unaware of these events. Over the next four months the gang continued raids, but gradually lost communication with Musgrove. Messengers continued to try to get through and were arrested one by one as Cook intercepted them. Reports of continued roundups of gang members came in from several territories. One of Musgrove's top aides, Jack Willetson, and two of his men were captured and lynched in New Mexico Territory. Five arrests in Texas, ten in southern Colorado Territory, and two more in Wyoming Territory hailed the demise of Musgrove's syndicate.

Musgrove's whereabouts, however, were still unknown. Some theorized that he had left the region entirely. Cook wasn't convinced of that. Then a report came in that several holdups had occurred in northern

Colorado Territory. Each had been perpetrated by one lone man. The descriptions of the bandit seemed to fit all accounts of Musgrove's appearance. Cook speculated that Musgrove had run out of money.

Soon Musgrove went back to horse stealing. He had crossed into Wyoming Territory for a night of several raids on small ranches. Musgrove then fled back into Colorado Territory. U.S. Marshal, H. D. Haskell, had been alerted by Cook to be on the lookout. Almost immediately, Haskell and his posse were in pursuit of Musgrove. Haskell's posse finally had Musgrove cornered in a rocky gulch along the Cache la Poudre River near Ft. Collins.

After Haskell kept Musgrove pinned down for twenty-four hours, Musgrove requested a truce to talk to the marshal. Haskell agreed and was allowed to walk into the hiding place, where he discovered that Musgrove had enough provisions to hold out for weeks. Haskell also noticed the stolen horses were hidden in a place where it was unlikely he could rescue them.

Musgrove offered to make a deal. He said Haskell could take back any stock he could identify on condition that the posse would then leave. Haskell accepted, and was able to verify ownership on most of the horses. Then he and the posse escorted the herd home. However, Haskell was not content to return without Musgrove. He sent most of the horses home with the posse, but separated some of them into a smaller herd. Hoping to draw Musgrove out, Haskell slowly meandered north pushing his part of the herd by himself. Sure enough, Musgrove followed and attempted to steal the horses at night when he thought Haskell was sleeping. Haskell was awake and waiting, and he easily captured Musgrove.

Another account of Musgrove's capture states that Abner Loomis of Fort Collins lived near the Cache la Poudre River at a place called Pleasant Valley. Loomis had known Musgrove lived in the area for years and also knew of his horse stealing. A deal had been struck between the two men, whereby Musgrove would not steal horses from the local farmers. If he did they would come after him and kill him. Supposedly Musgrove kept this agreement, but Loomis had a change of heart when he later learned that the whole region was after Musgrove. Loomis is said to have entrapped Musgrove and led him right into the hands of U.S. Marshal Haskell.

Though accounts of his capture may vary, it was Haskell who brought Musgrove into Denver and turned him over to Marshal Cook. After almost a year of work at putting an end to Musgrove and his gangs, Cook should have been overjoyed at the current situation. However, the date was early November and the courts did not reconvene until January. Cook knew he would have to hold Musgrove in jail until then, while many of Musgrove's gang was still at large. He believed it would be only a matter of time before a jailbreak would be attempted.

Sure enough many of the old Musgrove gang began to filter into Denver. Ed Franklin headed for the city when he heard of Musgrove's arrest. Franklin had been the assistant to Musgrove throughout the gang's successful raids earlier in the year. He met up with Sanford Duggan, another outlaw, and they both rode into Denver together. One of their first acts was to rob a man of $135. That man turned out to be Judge Brooks.

Judge Brooks informed Marshal Cook immediately. Cook put out the alert and was soon notified that the hoodlums had gone on to neighboring Golden. Cook set out for Golden immediately and, in a confrontation designed to arrest the men, an innocent man was killed, as well as Ed Franklin. Sanford Duggan escaped.

In Denver the next day, mob justice was underway. Word of Judge Brooks' holdup and the influx of Musgrove's gang members had alarmed and frightened the citizens. Adding this to the events that transpired in Golden the night before, the populace filled Denver streets and demanded the bandits leave town. Reports say that the huge crowds in the streets unnerved the Musgrove followers, who were holed up in the Holladay Street saloons and bordellos. Panicking, they retreated from the city in thirty minutes.

The crowd then headed for the county jail. The *Rocky Mountain News* reported that among the throng were doctors, merchants, professional people, and other prominent citizens. Amazingly, the mob moved along quietly with no shouting. It was orderly and determined. They held Musgrove responsible for all of the recent troubles.

Since the crowd was also well armed, their arrival was not met with resistance from the officers guarding the jail. By overwhelming agreement, the people removed Musgrove from his jail cell. He was then marched to the Larimer Street Bridge over Cherry Creek. Musgrove, observing the crowd around him, hoped for a last-ditch attempt to free him. But his cronies were nowhere to be seen.

A hangman's noose was suspended from the bridge. He only asked to have paper and pencil to write farewell notes to his wife in Cheyenne, and to his brother in Mississippi. He was given the materials and a few minutes to complete the letters. As he wrote, his legs were tied together. He was then hoisted into a wagon, which was positioned on the dry bed of Cherry Creek below the noose. Musgrove was defiant to the last as he supposedly smoked a cigarette, and then said: "Go on with your work." The noose was placed around his neck and the wagon was pulled from under him. It was November 24, 1868, and Musgrove was dead.

Ten days later, Sanford Duggan was finally captured in Cheyenne and brought back to Denver. Marshal Cook knew the mood of Denverites had not changed with the death of Musgrove. Duggan was considered part of the same problem. Although Cook tried to protect Duggan so he could stand trial, it is suspected the marshal's own men betrayed him. A lynching party learned of Cook's plan to move Duggan to an unknown location. Before the transfer could take place, Duggan was seized and hung from the limb of a nearby cottonwood tree.

Lee Musgrove's legacy was a death trail—including those he killed, the scores who died following him, and his own violent end.

Ike and Port Stockton, Rustlers & Robbers

By 1881, outlaw gangs were roaming the southwest Colorado and northern New Mexico Territory, stealing and killing, while the victimized residents were conducting their own vigilante lynchings to abate the criminal activity. On the tenth of January, Port Stockton, continuing his criminal ways, took over a widow's ranch in New Mexico Territory. He then moved into the lodgings with his wife and family.

The Stockmen's Protective Association was out to get Stockton, and rode to the cabin to confront him.

Meanwhile Port's brother, Ike Stockton, had retreated from a cattlemen's feud in New Mexico Territory and found refuge in nearby Colorado. Port was the most active outlaw of the two brothers, but the Stockmen's Protective Association final actions toward Port on that January day would change Ike into a full-time embittered hoodlum.

A great and cataclysmic encounter was occurring in southwestern Colorado in the 1870s and early 1880s. The towns of Animas City and Durango were competing for dominance. The Ute Indians were fighting to maintain their native rights of ownership. Mining was claiming the ground underneath the region as coal and gold ore rights were disputed. Railroad magnates were vying for the best routes to expand their realms, and cattlemen were fighting range wars. Lawless hoodlums were running wild, while decent citizens tried their best to contain them. In the midst of this chaotic atmosphere, the Stockton brothers managed to become involved in many of these clashes.

Isaac "Ike" Stockton and William Porter "Port" Stockton were born in Cleburne, Texas, in the early 1850s. They were said to be of good parentage and raised in religious homes. Although their youth was unremarkable, the townsfolk said they were decent boys.

When Port was on the threshold of adulthood, however, he was said to have killed someone. In a feud involving his girlfriend, Port had become jealous and killed his rival. At the time, Port still lived in his hometown. But this murder started him off on a life of running from the law. He left Cleburne to avoid arrest, and during the next several years, he traveled north through the Texas panhandle to New Mexico Territory and Kansas.

Port became known as a braggart who enjoyed being the center of attention. He liked to enter a saloon waving a revolver in each hand and demanding a drink. Or he would crash a dance hall party wearing his guns, when it had been posted that partygoers should leave their weapons at home.

Wildness was part of Port's demeanor. But he had another side to his character as well, and would occasionally settle down and take a regular job. He worked on cattle ranches and tended bar in saloons.

Sometime after Port left Texas, his brother Ike joined him. They were hired to herd cattle on the range between New Mexico and Colorado territories. There they met the Eskridge brothers and became involved in cattle rustling. While they were employed by a rancher, the Stockton-Eskridge gang would steal some of the cattle they were herding, rush them off to a hiding place across the border, and later sell them. It was a profitable scheme.

When cattle came up missing, the Stockton-Eskridge "employees" would readily join in with their employers to fight Indians who were blamed for the theft. If, by chance, other rustlers were suspected, the gang would "find evidence" that pointed to a neighboring ranch owner. This caused the stockowners to be divided against each other. Distrust kept them from joining forces and figuring out the real cause of their missing cattle. There was little cooperation and feuds were common.

Ike and Port traveled back and forth across the New Mexico Territory border regularly. They became familiar with the San Juan

Animas City, Colorado in 1880.
Denver Public Library, Western History Collection, X-6608

country in southwest Colorado Territory and the Shiprock area of northern New Mexico Territory. Knowledge of this region would become very useful in both of their futures.

Rustlers were not the only reason for the feuds among cattle ranchers. The vastness of the ranges on which the cattle roamed, as well as the lack of fences, resulted in constant encroachment issues with herds frequently wandering onto another rancher's land. Not only was pastureland trespassed, fields of corn and other plantings were often trampled by a neighbor's herd of cattle. There were not enough cowhands to control the herds. Those they did hire were often like the Stocktons and Eskridges, who stole from the owners. Sometimes the thieves really were the Indians who were retaliating for the loss of their land.

In the Brunot Treaty of 1873, the Utes had signed away their rights to the mining districts of the San Juan Mountains of Colorado Territory. Previous treaties had already diminished their native domain. It is unknown whether the tribes completely understood what they were giving up, but Chief Ouray had always been a proponent of forfeiting land rather than fighting. He thought he was saving the lives of his people. Although he may have been right, many of his tribe did not agree with him. Several assassination attempts were made on Ouray's life by his own tribesmen. Frustrated renegade Utes often fought with, and stole from, the ever-growing population of immigrants.

The Brunot Treaty opened the door to settlement and mining activities in southern Colorado Territory. By 1876, Animas City had grown slowly into a small settlement comprised of log buildings and cabins. It sat along the Animas River, named from the original Spanish "El Rio de las Animas Perdidas" meaning "the river of lost souls." It was also the gateway to the San Juan Mountains from where silver and gold had begun to flow. Port Stockton would eventually find his way to Animas City, but not until he had continued to build on his scathing reputation.

Two major cattle feuds, the Lincoln County War and the Colfax County War, had been taking place in northern New Mexico Territory. The Stocktons were friends with a family named Coe and fought on the same side during these cattle disputes. But in the mid-1870s, the constant feuding led Lou Coe to move to a new location near Farmington. He hoped to get away from the fighting, and his brothers joined him there. Ike Stockton, too, wanted to settle down and give up the cattle wars. He bought land near the Coe's in Farmington and began a ranching life. Eventually, he married and became a father of two children.

Port Stockton, however, was not ready to settle down. He left his brother in Farmington and traveled to Las Vegas, in New Mexico Territory, and then on to Raton and Trinidad, Colorado. The well-known old scout "Uncle Dick" Wootton told of one encounter he had with Port at his tollgate and eatery on Raton Pass. Port had heard that one of his friends had been killed over in Trinidad and he was out to revenge it. He slammed through the doors of Uncle Dick's café and had a revolver in each hand held up in the air. He yelled at the frightened occupants and demanded to know if his friend's killer was on the premises. He left in an angry temper and later mistakenly killed a man he thought to be his friend's murderer.

Port also took up with Clay Allison, another known desperado who alternately participated in local crimes and worked occasionally as a lawman. Together, they rustled cattle, robbed stages, and were generally wild outlaws.

Sometime during these years, Port was said to have settled in Animas City. He married and became the father of three children. He apparently had a home and possibly a ranch in the area, where he was still rustling cattle. Possibly he remained involved in other criminal activities as well.

In 1879, the Meeker Massacre pitted the Ute Indians against the Indian agent, Nathan Meeker, and the army. In the uprising, Meeker and others were killed. Fear of similar retaliation by the Indians led to the building of Fort Flagler at Animas City. It was also thought that more security would be achieved if the town hired a new marshal.

With the constant upheaval in the transient population, Indian uprisings, and varying degrees of lawlessness among the people, towns had difficulty keeping a permanent marshal. Most were ineffective, many ran off at the first sign of trouble, and some were outlaws themselves. Most towns knew little or nothing about the backgrounds of those they hired. In 1880, Animas City hired Port Stockton as the town marshal. He was, like so many others before him, temporarily able to keep the peace and run his office efficiently. As long as it suited him, he took the job seriously.

By summer though, a new wave of people came through town. Gold seekers poured in to take advantage of the warm weather in the mining areas. The town council posted an ordinance that no firearms were permitted within the town of Animas City. A new arrival named Captain Hart came into town wearing his gun belt, and Marshal Port Stockton halted him along the street. Hart claimed not to be aware of the law. An argument progressed into threats, and soon guns were drawn. Shots were fired and Hart dropped to the ground with a head wound. Although Hart recovered, Stockton's actions were questioned by some citizens. The local newspaper, however, defended the marshal in upholding the law. It was later learned that Stockton knew Hart from their earlier feuding days in New Mexico Territory, and there was "bad blood" between them.

Stockton did not fare so well in his next brutal incident. The town barber of Animas City was a Maori immigrant with a British accent. He had heard of Port's dealings with Captain Hart. When Stockton came into his shop one day for a shave, the barber was apparently nervous. His hands shook and when he ran the blade down the marshal's cheek, it nicked him. The marshal angrily jumped out of the chair. Seeing Stockton's reaction, the barber ran from the shop, but the marshal pursued him, firing his gun. The barber fell when he was wounded, and Stockton proceeded to beat the man's head and face with his gun.

Citizens who witnessed the shooting and beating were horrified. This time the town council decided Stockton had gone too far and wanted him arrested. The now "former" Marshal Stockton heard they were coming after him and fled to New Mexico Territory.

Meanwhile, Ike Stockton had been living on his ranch near Farmington, in New Mexico Territory. In spite of his desire to quit fighting cattle wars, he apparently gave in to his old ways of rustling. At the same time, he ran a supposedly legitimate ranching operation on his land. Another account says he stayed out of rustling, but the same problems of the fenceless range persisted. Eventually, Ike and his friend Lou Coe became enemies. Coe formed a group called the Stockmen's Protective Association to protect ranchers from horse and cattle rustlers. They turned into a vigilante group and started lynching anybody they suspected to be a thief. The dispute became known as the Farmington Feud.

Ike was starting to be concerned about the Stockmen's Protective Association and was hoping to avoid more cattle wars like the ones he had left behind in Lincoln and Colfax counties. Late in 1880, he decided to move his family north to Animas City, Colorado, to get away from the problems that were arising in New Mexico Territory. About this time, the new town of Durango, Colorado was beginning to supplant Animas

City as the leading city of the area. The Denver and Rio Grande Railroad had established Durango as the center of its rail system. Animas City was just 2 miles north and in sight of Durango. But local residents and businesses wanted to be closer to the railroad and Animas City eventually went into decline.

Port Stockton arrived back in New Mexico Territory after his mishaps in Animas City. Port was still a reckless cowboy, but he had to find a place for his family to live. He found an old widow's cabin on a ranch, which she had temporarily vacated to visit a relative. Her hired man was overseeing the ranch in her absence. Port decided to take over the place, and killed the hired man in the effort. Port and his family moved into the home.

On January 10, 1881, the Stockmen's Protective Association heard about Port's takeover of the widow's ranch. Coe and his gang, who were now enemies of the Stocktons, closed in on Port at the cabin. There, Port and Coe had an argument. As a result, Port is said to have been shot to death in the doorway of the cabin. His wife was wounded. The children were apparently unharmed since no word is mentioned about them in any report.

Ike Stockton, who had tried to stay out of the feud, was now outraged and embittered over the death of his brother and the wounding of Port's wife. Ike felt he could no longer stay out of the fray. He formed a group of several men, including Clay Allison, and rode into New Mexico Territory to go after the Stockmen's Protective Association. A shootout occurred, and Ike's gang stole cattle and returned across the border with them.

By now, the long history of these border feuds had caught the attention of the governors of both Colorado and New Mexico Territory. They agreed to cooperate in extraditing outlaws across the state borders for trial. Governor Lew Wallace of New Mexico Territory announced rewards for the capture of a long list of known feud participants. The amount of $500 was offered for Ike Stockton, and $250 was offered for Clay Allison.

Since Allison was on the list, he had to give up his badge as sheriff of Conejos County. He then decided to become a full-fledged outlaw. He and Stockton and some of his men robbed the Sanderson-Barlowe Stage and got away with $600 in currency, four gold watches, and $2,400 in drafts. Other robberies purported to involve Stockton and Allison were reported all across southern Colorado.

Meanwhile, the Farmington Feud continued. One morning in April, the Stockmen's Protective Association showed up in Durango. They were led by Lou Coe and his brothers. Stockton's gang intercepted them and a battle raged on the mesa directly east of town. Bullets from all the gunfire were said to have hailed down over the citizens on the main streets of Durango. None of the local populace was hurt, and both gangs eventually gave up fighting and rode off in another unfinished skirmish. The Farmington gang returned over the border into New Mexico Territory.

In the midst of all this unease, a clash with the Utes known as the "Battle of Little Castle Valley" began on June 1, 1881. Ranchers dead bodies were found in an area where these men had been holding a string of horses. The horses were gone, money had been taken, and Ute Indians were said to be spending lots of money in town—buying new hats. Ike Stockton and men from all over the San Juan Basin joined the posse to go after the Indians. By the time the men were organized, the Utes were long gone into the mountains. The posse decided to pursue the Utes, who were far more familiar with the terrain, and the Indians held off the men's posse with ease. Stockton, though, was said to be one of the best fighters in the battle by the time it was over.

Ike Stockton stayed out of New Mexico Territory, since almost everyone was on the lookout for him there. He and his gang also spent most of their time away from Durango, except when Ike made short visits to his family. One afternoon, the gang was having a wild time at a saloon in nearby Silverton, a mountain mining town at 10,000 feet in altitude. Full of the spirits they'd been drinking and additionally affected by the altitude, their drunken joviality spilled out onto the streets. Soon they were shooting off their guns and shattering the streetlights, along with everything else in sight. The town marshal responded to the mayhem of the gang, but was killed when a stray bullet struck him.

The gang fled town. The Silverton citizens were set on revenge and offered a $2,500 reward for the killer. That was a huge amount of money in those days, and Ike Stockton couldn't resist. The bullet that struck and killed the Silverton marshal was random and it would have been impossible to know whose gun had fired it. Stockton decided the folks in Silverton would never know exactly who fired the fatal shot. Unless, of course, Stockton said he knew.

Purely for the reward, Ike decided to turn in one of his own gang. He led Silverton lawmen and a posse to Burt Wilkinson, who had been with Stockton at the saloon on the day of the shooting. Ike identified Wilkinson as the man who fired the bullet at the marshal. The reward went to Stockton. As soon as the posse left town, Wilkinson was lynched by a Silverton mob.

Despite some peoples' support of Ike Stockton in various situations, many knew he had been willing to sacrifice one of his own men to get the reward. This was such a dishonorable affront to the local citizenry that they could not allow it. The Durango sheriff and his deputy were ordered by the city council to arrest Stockton.

When Ike and a friend came into Durango one day, the lawmen approached Ike and told him he was under arrest. He grabbed for his gun, but the marshal and his deputy fired first. Stockton was shot twice, once in the lower leg and once in the hip.

He didn't die until the next morning. The bones in his leg had been shattered and even though his leg was amputated, doctors were unable to save him. It was October 26, 1881 and Ike was probably about thirty years old.

Newspapers had reported Port's death earlier in the same year. He was probably about twenty-eight years old. Now they reported Ike's death. Neither of the brothers received much of a write-up, and Durango was glad to be rid of them.

Alfred Packer, Cannibal

On August 3, 1886, the *Rocky Mountain News* reported the ongoing testimony in the trial of Alfred Packer:

Packer's manner while on the stand was very excited. He detailed his trip, his act of cannibalism, his arrival at Los Pinos Agency, his arrest and subsequent escape from Saguache, his wanderings up to 1883, and his final capture at Fort Fetterman, in a wild, incoherent manner, standing in his shirt-sleeves, waving his mutilated hand in the air and haranguing the jury in broken sentences.

He frequently cursed his enemies in very plain words, and refused to be governed by his counsel. Replying once to a remonstrance on their part, he said, "You shut up. I'm on the stand now."

The trial lasted for three days and the jury reached its verdict in just three hours.

Alfred G. Packer was born on November 21, 1842, in Allegheny County, Pennsylvania. Epilepsy was the scourge of his childhood and was a little understood malady at that time. Consequently, young Packer was often socially ostracized from his peers. He and his family—which included his parents, two sisters, and a brother—were members of the Quaker religion.

It is unclear why he left home at an early age, but his medical condition may have played a part in his desire to escape harassment. Some said his own family sent him away due to their misunderstanding of, and inability to deal with, his illness. He was able to serve a short apprenticeship with a printer while trying to hide his condition. Besides the epileptic fits that ravaged him, some side effects included a quarrelsome nature and a high-pitched, shrill voice.

In 1862, at the age of twenty, Packer decided to enlist in the army to fight in the Civil War. When he joined the 16th U.S. Infantry in Winona, Minnesota, his record indicates he was 5 feet 8½ inches tall, of light complexion, with blue eyes and light hair. His occupation was recorded as shoemaker. Although he had been christened with the first name of Alfred, he preferred "Alferd" and had this name tattooed on his right arm along with the name of his encampment, "Camp Thomas," and his battalion and infantry numbers. Just eight months later, he was discharged "as incapable of performing the duties of a soldier because of epilepsy."

Records show that Packer re-enlisted in Ottumwa, Iowa, six months after his discharge. Nearly a year later he was discharged again due to his epilepsy. The army surgeon stated that Packer's epileptic seizures occurred "once in 48 hours and sometimes as often as two or three times in 48 hours."

Alfred drifted from job to job. He worked as a hunter, hard rock miner, trapper, teamster, and guide. He had also begun to invent certain facts about his life and work experience, which was unsteady due to his epileptic episodes. In 1873, when Packer was thirty-one years old, he settled in Georgetown, in Colorado Territory, where a mining accident caused the loss of parts of his index and little finger on his left hand. He then moved on to Sandy, in Utah Territory, and worked in a smelter that processed ore from Bingham Canyon. By then the medical world had discovered that bromides could be helpful to epileptics, and Packer is said to have used them whenever possible.

Later the same year he heard news of rich ore discoveries in the mountains of Colorado Territory. A group of gold-seeking miners was

Alfred G. Packer as a young man.
CO Historical Society, F33253

forming at Bingham to travel into the San Juan Mountains. Packer joined up with them, and although they said they had limited knowledge of the Colorado mountains, Packer claimed he was very familiar with the area.

By the fall of 1873 Alfred Packer and the group of twenty-one men headed for the Colorado border, along with horses, wagons, and provisions. Early in their journey it became apparent that they had brought insufficient provisions. Feed intended for the livestock began to be used for the men. Their travel was slow, the weather brought early snow, and game became scarce. As they reached the border, they encountered the Ute Indians, who led them to the camp of Chief Ouray, near present-day Delta, Colorado. The group was allowed to stay with Ouray, where they were provided shelter and warmth, as well as the opportunity to trade with the Indians.

Winter had settled in and Chief Ouray warned against proceeding into the high mountains. But many of the men in Packer's group were restless. Those without wagons and teams eventually decided to forge ahead. Two groups were organized, with one group traveling ahead separately. That left six men in the second group and they began their foray into the mountains on February 9, 1874. Besides Packer, the members of this expedition included "Old man" Swan, George Noon, James Humphrey, Frank Miller, and Shannon Wilson Bell.

Chief Ouray had provided directions to Saguache, in Colorado Territory, in the heart of the San Juans about 100 miles southeast. He told them of a "cow camp" which was "seven suns away" where provisions could be acquired and instructed them to follow the creek from there to the Los Pinos Indian Agency. After that it was just 40 more miles to their destination.

The first group became lost immediately. They struggled for three weeks before reaching the government cattle camp and were near starvation when they arrived. With new provisions they continued on through raging and turbulent winter storms and finally arrived at Los Pinos, barely alive.

The second group of six men, Packer's group, was last seen headed southeast as they disappeared into a snowstorm.

It would be two months before Packer would emerge from the frozen wilderness and encounter a man who was out gathering firewood. It was mid-April, and Packer's matted hair and beard obviously revealed that he had suffered long exposure to severe weather.

Packer's first words are said to be: "Is this the agency?" He was led to the mess hall, where he met other agency employees. It is documented that Packer could not eat their food at first, and that he related his story of having been separated from his group and left behind. He claimed to have had to proceed on his own after that. The other five men had not shown up at the agency.

For Packer, all might have ended happily right there. However, as he talked more to others about his experience his story began to change. Those who questioned him were told different versions, which varied wildly. And soon, other travelers arrived who had been part of the original group that had stayed behind at Chief Ouray's camp. They recognized Packer and wondered how he had acquired the knife that belonged to Frank Miller. Packer also had money, which they knew he had not possessed when they were last with him.

With no evidence to back up any of his stories, Packer came under suspicion. But there was also no proof of what was fast becoming the generally held belief among the community: that Packer was involved in "foul play" regarding the men in his group, who had still not shown up.

Under pressure from more questioning, Packer finally revealed a new scenario. He told of the starvation and exposure which had led to the death of four of the men along the way. The fifth man, Bell, had attacked Packer, and in self-defense Packer killed Bell with a hatchet. He then revealed how he had survived by cannibalizing the bodies. Packer maintained his innocence in the deaths of his companions, even though he now admitted freely to the cannibalism.

The Indian agent, Charles Adams, thought Packer's story could be proved if the bodies could be found. He asked Packer to lead a search party back to the location where the men had last been seen. Packer agreed and led the group into the wilderness, where he became lost and said he could not remember how to reach the spot. Many in the search party were convinced of Packer's guilt.

Because of these grave suspicions, Packer was incarcerated in a makeshift jail in Saguache without any charges against him. Weeks later, the bodies of the five men were discovered together below a cliff with obvious hatchet wounds in their skulls. They each showed signs of having been cannibalized. Pieces of the bodies had been cut from legs, foreheads, and torsos. An empty bromide tin was also found at the scene.

A warrant for the arrest of Packer was finally issued. In one of several odd twists that would occur in this drama, Packer managed to escape before the warrant could be served. He would not be seen again for almost ten years.

In 1883 a man using the name of John Schwartze was seen at Fort Fetterman near Cheyenne, in Wyoming Territory. The man was Alfred Packer, who had been living under an assumed name. He was recognized and turned in to law enforcement agents by one of his old acquaintances from the original gold-seeking band in Bingham, in Utah Territory. Packer did not resist his arrest.

Packer then decided that he wanted to make a new statement about what had happened during that tragic winter in the San Juans. This time his story portrayed a group of hopeless men, sick and hungry from the cold and snow. Unable to find food, Packer said the men were "crying and praying." One of the men asked him to go up on a hilltop to see if he could see anything. Another man was acting crazy. When Packer returned, he found the crazy man sitting by the fire roasting something on a stick. He saw one body with its skull crushed in by the hatchet. The other three men had also been struck in the forehead with the hatchet. When the crazy man saw Packer, he came at him swinging the hatchet.

Packer then shot him in the side, grabbed the hatchet, and struck him on the top of his head. Although Packer says he tried every day to get out of the camp, the snow-covered terrain and blizzard conditions made it impossible. So he stayed in the camp and ate the flesh of the dead men to stay alive. Eventually the weather allowed passage out so he could hike to the Los Pinos Indian Agency.

Packer also provided limited information about how he escaped from the Saguache jail and what he did for the ten years until his recapture. He says he was passed a key made of a knife blade, which unlocked the irons that shackled him. He fled to Pueblo, where he worked on a nearby ranch and later rented the ranch and grew a crop of corn. He moved on to Arizona Territory and eventually traveled to Wyoming Territory.

Packer's arrest became sensational news. He was tried for murder in April of 1883 at the Hinsdale County Courthouse in Lake City, Colorado. Alferd Packer decided to represent himself without benefit of a defense lawyer.

The prosecution held that Packer's motivation for the murder of his companions had been sheer greed. He had shown up at the Indian agency with considerable amounts of money and the wallet of one of the victims. The act of cannibalism was not given much attention in the trial. It was apparently thought that this occurred only as an after-thought for the purpose of survival and Packer's real interest was the money these men had carried with them.

One witness who was called to testify was Otto Mears, known as the "Pathfinder of the San Juan" because he built roadways and railroads through the area's precipitous mountains. He owned real estate all along the road he had built between Saguache and Lake City, and also ran a supply store in Saguache. He said he sold a horse, bridle, and sad-dle to Packer after he had left the Indian Agency. Packer had seemed to be throwing his money around indiscriminately and paid about $100 cash for the livery items. Otto recollected seeing the additional wallet, which he called a "pocketbook." He also saw other items enclosed in it, including a Wells Fargo bank draft. The possession of this draft was considered key to Packer's guilt.

Alfred Packer was outraged by Mears' testimony and maintained he did not have the draft. "Otto Mears swears that he saw a Wells Fargo Bank Draft," Packer said, "and before I get through I will prove that Mears told a lie." He lost his temper at this point and rose from his chair, threatening to kill Mears at his first opportunity. It took considerable effort to restrain Packer and calm him down before the trial could proceed.

The jury was not persuaded by Packer's defense of himself. He had often rambled and his demands were largely ignored. It took only three hours of deliberation before the jury returned its verdict. Packer was convicted of murder.

However, another bizarre twist occurred when it was discovered that the state of Colorado had no law regarding murder. The legislature had repealed the original 1870 murder statute without providing a new one in its place. Packer's crime had taken place after the repeal of the murder statute.

He was transferred to the town of Gunnison to await a ruling, since it was feared a lynching party might overpower the Lake City law enforcement officials. Packer sat imprisoned in the Gunnison County jail for three years before the judgment was finally made. The Colorado Supreme Court remanded the case for a new trial, stating that Packer could not be tried for murder since there had been no established punishment at the time for this crime. He could be tried, however, for the crime of manslaughter. A new defense on Packer's behalf argued that his rights had been violated by his lengthy confinement during the delay for the ruling. This was overruled.

In 1886 a new trial was set. Much of the same information was covered again, only this time Otto Mears was said to be unavailable. The record of his original testimony was read to the court instead. Some felt that Mears was afraid of Packer's earlier threat to kill him, and so he stayed away from the second trial.

This time Packer was convicted of manslaughter and sentenced to forty years of hard labor at the state penitentiary in Cañon City. It became the most severe sentence ever handed down for manslaughter in American history. Many felt the sentence was overly harsh considering the lack of provable evidence.

This might finally have been the end of it, except that Packer's second conviction was appealed several times between 1886 and 1898. Each time, the Colorado Supreme Court rejected the appeal, and each time Packer gained more support from the public. In 1899, *The Denver Post* appointed their most heralded reporter, Mrs. Leonel Ross O'Bryan (known humorously as "Polly Pry") to take on the story as her only assignment. For the next two years she used the newspaper's influence to hound Governor Charles S. Thomas to either parole or pardon Packer.

Thomas was said to be a close friend of Otto Mears, the man who had given damaging testimony in the Packer case. Mrs. O'Bryan wrote that Mears was afraid of Packer being released and she labeled him a "COWARD." She accused the governor for being influenced by Mears instead of doing the right thing.

Governor Thomas resisted almost to the end of his political career. In 1901, as the final act of his outgoing term and on his last day in office, Thomas pardoned Packer.

Having served fifteen years of his sentence, Packer was finally free. He moved to a ranch in Littleton, south of Denver, and lived for another six years. In April of 1907, Alfred Packer died at the age of sixty-five. His grave is located in the Littleton cemetery, where Packer was buried with full military honors. The gravestone displays his given name "Alfred Packer," and lists his infantry unit from his first enlistment.

Years after the death of Packer, former Governor Thomas wrote a letter to the newspaper at Lake City. For the first time he publicly related his thoughts about Packer, and explained his reluctance in granting the pardon. Thomas stated that the letters Packer had written during his incarceration in Lake City and Gunnison were shared with him by local officials who censored the inmate's mail. Apparently, Packer wrote to his sister and other family members in Pennsylvania, blaming them for his terrible life. The letters, which expressed his rage and anger in the most foul and profane language imaginable, astonished the governor. Also of great concern were Packer's threats toward his relatives, which he said he would carry out upon his release. Governor Thomas had been asked not to reveal this information publicly. He had decided to visit Packer while he was in jail, and said that he did so several times, during which he

Alfred Packer gravestone.
CO Historical Society, #F37188

talked with him at length. Thomas saw no redeeming qualities in Packer's nature and felt the inmate's attitude had not improved. Only because of Packer's failing health did the governor finally agree to a pardon. But he stipulated this release upon the condition that Packer would not be allowed to leave the state of Colorado for the rest of his life. This was done to protect Packer's family members.

Packer's notoriety has continued long beyond his death. In the mid–1960s, the University of Colorado student body voted to rename the student union eatery, "The Alferd G. Packer Grill." And in the 1990s, a cookbook was published called *Alferd Packer's High Protein Cookbook*. It featured recipes using wild game meats.

On Memorial Day of 2004, the 700 residents of Lake City held the Alferd Packer Days festival, including bone-tossing competitions and mystery meat barbecues. During that summer, the still-standing Hinsdale County Courthouse was regularly packed with tourists for the weekly re-enactment of Packer's trial. *The Denver Post* reported one town citizen as saying, "Some people think it's gross, but there's still so much interest."

"Soapy" Smith, Con Man

Use this soap and wash your sins away! Cleanliness is next to godliness, but the feel of good crisp greenbacks in the pocket is paradise itself. Step right up friends, and watch me closely.

With these words, "Soapy" Smith drew a crowd along a busy Denver street in 1888. Onlookers witnessed as he held up a $100 bill, placed it around a small bar of soap, wrapped them together in colorful paper, and tossed the package into a pile in front of him. Next, he enclosed a $50 bill with another bar, wrapped it, and added it to the pile. He repeated this again and again, placing large bills in each package until the pile grew large. Sometimes Smith made it very obvious when he didn't place any money in with a bar or two, and most people watching thought they knew for sure which packages contained the big bills.

"Soapy" offered his audience a chance to buy the wrapped soaps for only $5 each. He admitted this was a "ridiculous price if you only got a 5-cent bar of soap," but he reminded his viewers, "you have to take a chance if you want to win big!"

The crowd was reluctant, but one man eagerly stepped up, put his $5 on the table, and chose from the pile. When he opened the wrapper he found a $100 bill folded inside with the soap. Everyone saw his joyful reaction as he jumped up and down holding up his newly won prize. Others immediately crowded forward to pay their $5, expecting to win too. This time, however, the players opened the wrappers and found only soap.

In actuality, the first "winner" was an employee of Soapy's and knew which bar of soap held the prize. Smith's experienced sleight-of-hand made it appear that money had been placed in nearly all the other soap packages, when in reality, he had palmed the large bills so none were included. Soapy Smith had, once again, tricked his audience and swindled a few more poor suckers in early Denver.

Born in 1860 to a family in Noonan, Georgia, Jefferson Randolph Smith had an early life that could not have predicted his future "career" as a con man. His father and uncles were all well-educated aristocrats, and he was raised in the lifestyle of southern landowners. Following the Civil War the family moved to Texas. There, Smith became a cowhand as a young man while he pondered his future. His parents hoped he would choose law or the ministry.

The rough life of the range didn't appeal to Smith, but it did bring him into contact with the local gambling halls of San Antonio. His sharp mind easily grasped the finesse required to win at the poker tables, and he discovered the excitement of winning by his wits.

When the circus came to town young Smith found something even more exciting than poker. A man named Clubfoot Hall was operating his shell game outside the big tent. Hall would quickly circulate a dried green pea under three walnut shell halves while the crowd watched. When he stopped the rotation, a player would bet on which shell hid the pea. Unknown to the bettor, Hall had palmed the pea at the last moment guaranteeing that it would never be under the selected shell. Occasionally, Hall would let someone win to keep the crowd interested.

Smith was completely dazzled. When he found out how it was done, he decided that this was the way he wanted to earn his living. By the mid-1880s, with guidance from Clubfoot Hall, he became skilled at his own shell-game pitch. He set up the game in front of a saloon or gambling house where he could entice passersby to test their eyes against his quick hands. Big profits filled his pockets as he cheerfully fleeced anyone willing to lay down their hard-earned cash.

Moving on to Houston, then through towns in Kansas, Smith finally decided to target Colorado. He had heard that the ore fields there were filled with hundreds of gambling houses and plenty of unsuspecting men with pockets full of silver and gold. It would be a con man's dream.

In 1885, Smith's first stop in Colorado was Leadville, where he immediately set up his shell game along the crowded streets. The miners were receptive to his likeable manner and were happily entertained by his quick hands. When they lost their money to him, they walked away shaking their heads in disbelief, thinking he was just too fast to beat!

Smith decided to grow a beard to blend into the community and to make himself look older than his twenty-five years. He was making plenty of money and also making friends among those he fleeced. Things were going even better in Leadville than he had imagined.

Smith's future reputation as "the best con man in Colorado" had barely begun and he was already thinking ahead to bigger possibilities. "Old Man Taylor" was running another shell game in town, and was said to be the "King of 'Em All" among con men. He operated at the corner of Third Street and Harrison, and Smith went to observe him. Taylor was the best Smith had ever seen, and he realized that his own youthful charisma, balanced with the old man's skills, would make a great team.

Smith used his smooth talk and personality to convince Taylor that teamwork would bring them both more profits. In just one trial, Smith proved that his lively banter helped to increase both the crowd and the winnings. Besides being paid a share of the income, Smith wanted Taylor to teach him all of his tricks. He agreed.

The shell game was gradually being taken over by more and more operators in town and Taylor's expertise led to a brand new scheme. He showed it to Smith, who was soon playing the shill for the soap con. Smith would brag to the locals about the bar of soap with the $100 bill wrapped inside, which he'd won off of an old man down the street. Then he would direct them there. The crowds grew large and money poured in for Smith and Taylor.

Old Man Taylor began to think about retiring and going to be with his sister in Minneapolis, so Smith gradually took over running the business. This provided the impetus for Smith to start thinking about expanding his influence and increasing his fortunes. He decided to move to Denver.

Although gambling and prostitution were legal across most of the West, con scams were borderline. They were considered small-time antics and were mostly overlooked if no one complained too much. When Smith set up his soap scheme at 17th and Larimer in Denver, the police were busy with more violent crimes. Ever the great showman, Smith operated from a fancy horse and buggy so he would be easily noticed along the busy streets.

It was in Denver that Smith began to be called "Soapy." The locals were referring, of course, to his soap scheme. Even the police, who wrote him up occasionally, filed their reports using the name "Soapy" Smith. Never detained long at the police station, he would just move his horse and buggy down the street to a new location.

Profits rolled in for "Soapy" and he began to befriend the police by convincing them that his schemes were only set up to swindle the outsiders visiting Denver, never the local citizens. City officials were won over by his style and natural charm, and sometimes by his financial contributions. By the late 1880s, Soapy Smith opened a gambling hall and was also beginning a new era as one of the kingpins of illegal activities in Denver.

It was time for Soapy to start protecting his business. His powers of persuasion helped bring other con men into a new organization he was forming, including Doc Baggs, Canada Bill, and "Reverend" Bowers. They along with other colorfully named members such as Yank Fewclothes, "Dolly" Brooks, and Icebox Murphy all answered to Soapy. When new con men came to Denver they were given a choice: join Soapy's group or leave Denver. He was not above using violence against any interloper.

The gang of con men grew so large that Soapy was called "The King of the Con." His friendly connections with politicians allowed him to run his operations from the city's finest Windsor Hotel and his Arcade Saloon. He later ran the Tivoli Saloon and Gambling Hall. The police department often reported to him if there were any arrests of his con men. A word from Soapy, to the right person, got them discharged.

Soapy Smith had steered clear of women during his early adult years. His upbringing in a strict religious home, as well as his total absorption in his shady business dealings, kept him from dallying with the ladies. But one night at a Denver concert, he was smitten with a singer named Anna (Addie) Nielsen. An overzealous, drunken man approached her after the performance and was so obnoxious that Soapy, in a fit of temper, beat the man profusely.

After a short courtship, Soapy married Addie. They later had three children, with one son christened Jefferson Randolph Smith. Soapy's marriage was kept very quiet and separate from his public life, and his children were totally sheltered from his underworld activities.

Soapy was known for his style, courtesy, and charisma, but he was also known for his quick, hot temper. Besides the earlier row over his future wife, his temper got him into many other skirmishes. One evening in 1889 he was losing a lot of money while gambling. It was a lifelong weakness, and once he started playing he could not bear to stop with a loss. To avoid this, he bet his watch to stay in the game. When his luck turned and he began to win again, he wanted to buy the watch back, but he was refused. His temper raged in response, and he drew a knife on the dealer and held it to his throat until the watch was returned.

Still, he was known to be one of Denver's most charitable residents. He handed out turkeys to the poor, and helped destitute families who traveled to Denver and arrived at Union Station to meet husbands and fathers who never picked them up. He bought return tickets for young women "of the street" who wanted to go back home, and provided a decent burial for those who had committed suicide. Many people were aware of Soapy's good deeds and often brought the needy to him, knowing he would help them.

Despite his charity, numerous articles in the *Rocky Mountain News* began to threaten Soapy's hold on Denver. One recounted a Sunday afternoon incident in Logan Park, where several members of Soapy's gang swindled picnickers who were out with their families. The shell game cheated many of them out of their money, and these innocent folks began to complain loudly. It evolved into pushing and shoving and a near-riot. The *Rocky Mountain News* named Soapy Smith as the culprit, although he allegedly was not there at the time.

Smith continued his drive for power by branching out into other lawless activities. He soon added burglars and robbers to his gang. New revenues filled his pockets when he offered protection to visiting businessmen from his own gang of thieves. "Father of the Protection Racket" would be another label he earned. Cash was flowing to him from nearly every sector of crime.

In the meantime, the *Rocky Mountain News* carried on its campaign against Soapy with more unflattering newspaper articles. They even explained how his con games worked, exposing him as a fraud.

Soapy reacted angrily by marching over to the newspaper offices to look for Colonel John Arkins, president of the printing company. When he found him, he began a fight and hit Arkins over the head with his cane. The Colonel fell to the ground and Soapy hit him again and again. He also kicked him a couple of times before leaving him there.

The *Rocky Mountain News* and the citizens of Denver considered Soapy's actions to be attempted murder. He was arrested and bailed out for $1,000, but was never brought to trial. The newspaper, however, wrote that Soapy Smith was "near the end of his rope."

The resulting publicity created problems for Soapy and his wife. She decided to move the family back to St. Louis where her parents lived. It was intended to be a temporary move, but although Soapy visited her there from time to time, she never returned.

Eventually the people of Denver began to tire of Soapy's shady activities and bad behavior. He moved his headquarters to nearby Edgewater's "White Front Saloon" on the outskirts of the city. The *Rocky Mountain News* persisted, however, in writing articles about his continued stronghold and protection by the Edgewater police.

With Soapy's operation in Denver becoming more difficult, he began to look for new opportunities elsewhere. The mountain gold-fields continued to produce brand new towns whenever a rich new strike was discovered. In 1892 such a place came into being almost overnight. Creede, Colorado was in the southwestern part of the state near Alamosa. Miner Nicholas Creede had found a pure vein of silver, and fortune hunters poured into the area from all over the country. The population soon rose to 10,000. Nearby camps included Jimtown, Weaver, Amethyst, Wasson, and Bachelor.

Soapy set out to explore the possibilities of moving to Creede. He found it to be a lawless town that he and his gang could take over almost effortlessly. He planned to be the "underworld king" of Creede. Within a month after he had established himself there, he made it known that he was now in charge.

The Orleans Club was soon built by Smith. This gambling house served as his headquarters and, despite two major fires that destroyed most of Creede that year, his club survived. The town was immediately rebuilt and included forty saloons.

Soapy's way of intertwining himself into both sides of the law revealed itself once again. While he was taking payoffs from the criminal sector, he also was pleased to have the opportunity to be the charitable leader for the law abiding decent folks. He suggested that Creede establish a government, and he offered to control the "rough element." His offer was gladly accepted, and within a few weeks he sent for his brother-in-law from Texas to be the new town marshal.

Bob Ford was about the only nemesis for Soapy when he arrived in Creede. Ford ran the dance hall and lived above it with his wife. He disliked Smith's assumed authority over the town. But Bob Ford had his own uneasy relationship with the townspeople. They knew he had killed Jesse James in Missouri several years earlier when he had been associated with the James gang. Instead of being a hero for his act, as he had intended, he had instead been shunned and derided almost everywhere he went. Jesse James had been a folk-hero outlaw to many, and Ford had shot him in the back, which made matters even worse. Bob Ford became a heavy drinking, bad-tempered man with a chip on his shoulder, and had moved to Creede to try to re-establish himself.

Smith dealt with Ford by meeting secretly with him. Nobody knew for sure whether Soapy threatened him with potential trouble from the gang, or if his smooth talk was enough, but Bob Ford never publicly spoke against Soapy again.

There were questions, though, about Soapy's possible involvement when Bob Ford was finally gunned down by Ed Kelly. Some said Kelly had his reasons to dislike Ford, but he shot and killed him in broad daylight on Creede's busy Main Street in front of numerous witnesses. He had been handed the gun from a man on horseback as Ford strode along the street. Even though Ford was not a town favorite, the citizens were outraged at this cold-blooded murder.

When a mob formed at the scene, ready to lynch Kelly, it was Soapy Smith who ran to his aid. He addressed the crowd to plead for law and order. The throng quieted and Soapy prevailed, as he so often did. Kelly was later legally tried and sent to prison. Only rumors were able to connect Soapy to Ford's death.

Creede continued to be under Soapy's spell. While he was extracting payments from newcomers to allow them to start businesses in town, and collecting from them for protection from his gang, he also continued to be a benevolent, charitable citizen who was generally liked and respected.

Several accounts tell of another of Soapy's outlandish cons. He acquired an oversized cement human figure, which he said had been dug up from the mountain above Creede. True to his showman nature, Soapy masterminded a plan to show off "Colonel Stone" as a prehistoric, petrified giant. He drew the crowd to a room decorated as a tomb, where the eerie figure lay. People, and their money, poured in for the "educational" lecture and viewing of the giant. Soapy profited again when P. T. Barnum put the figure in his traveling show.

By the mid-1890s rumors spread that silver prices were threatened, because the United States was considering using only gold to back up the country's money, discontinuing its use of silver entirely. Seeing the inevitable, Soapy knew this probability forecast a "bust" for Creede's mostly silver-based mining. He pulled one more con by "salting" a claim with rich ore before selling it to two Easterners for $2,500. Then he went back to Denver.

Soapy was not welcomed in Denver except by a few leftover corrupt politicians. New politicians had been elected to clean up the vice and crime in the capital city. Smith ended up in a standoff at City Hall, trying to dissuade the local officials from being so insistent about ridding the city of the "small-time" con games. Denver citizens stubbornly supported their leaders who wanted Soapy and his lawless friends to leave. He finally accepted the end to his reign in Colorado and left Denver in 1897, taking his gang with him. He had set his sights on another gold field.

This time he established headquarters in Skagway, Alaska, and for a short while Soapy's schemes worked as they had in Denver and Creede. But just like the "boom and bust" of the West's many mining towns, his life was about to go "bust." His overpowering manner had become maniacal. In an attempt to stop a newly formed vigilante group from opposing him as the "crime boss," Soapy exchanged gunfire with them and he was killed. It was July 8, 1898 and Soapy Smith was only thirty-eight years old.

Denver's newspapers reported Soapy's death, and although long stories were written about him, none expressed sadness about his loss. One echo of his brash life occurred nearly one hundred years after he had lived in Denver. A bar opened there on a downtown street in the 1980s, and was named "Soapy Smith's."

Jim Clark, Outlaw Marshal

While he was the marshal of Telluride, Jim Clark happily recounted this story to his friend, Cyrus Wells Shores, sheriff of Gunnison, saying, "The fellers who held up the bank were friends of mine. They told me their plans and said that if I made a point of being out of town at the time of the robbery they would give me a fair share of the take. They agreed to hide it under a big log along the trail on which they planned to make their getaway. They were true to their word and left me this roll of bills amounting to about $2,200." He then used part of the money to buy his friend a box of cigars.

Jim Clark was born around 1841 in Clay County, Missouri. Clark was the last name of his stepfather, the only father Jim could remember. His real father had the last name of Cummings, but he died when Jim was too young to remember. Jim's mother remarried and took the name of Clark for both herself and her son.

During Jim's teen years he reportedly teamed up with another local boy and stole his stepfather's mule. They ran away, riding the mule all the way to San Antonio, Texas where they sold the mule for money and bought some fancy western clothes, boots, and a pair of good six-shooters. The boys proceeded to hold up a stockman outside of town and took $1,400 from him. Afterwards, they returned home where Jim was rejected by his stepfather, but welcomed by his mother.

The Clark family later moved to Jackson County, Missouri. They occasionally took in boarders, including one man by the name of William Quantrill, who had come from Ohio to teach school in the area.

He became good friends with the Clarks, and Jim especially took a liking to him. No one knew at the time how Quantrill was soon to affect Jim's future.

In the mid-1850s Quantrill's brother wrote and asked him to travel to California with him. William left the school for a short time to make the trip. At this same time, the Civil War was looming in the country's near future and states had already taken sides in the dispute over slavery. Missouri was a slave state, but Kansas chose to be a free state.

On their way to California, William Quantrill and his brother traveled from Missouri into Kansas. There had been constant battles along the borders between the two states. The Kansans, or "Jayhawkers," would ride into Missouri, steal slaves, and take them back to Kansas to set them free. The "Border Ruffians" of Missouri fought against this practice and retaliated by stealing the slaves back. Many citizens of both states were killed in the resulting skirmishes.

The Quantrill brothers were caught in the middle of one such attack by General Lane's division of the Jayhawkers. William's brother was killed, and William himself was severely wounded and lay dying in a desolate location. He probably would have died had it not been for an old Indian who found him and nursed him back to health.

Quantrill returned to Jackson County and to the Clarks, and was able to finish the school year. He remained enraged by what had happened to him and his brother, and his only desire was to get revenge. What could one man do by himself to get back at these killers? He came up with a plan that would allow him to avenge his brother's death. He went to Leavenworth, Kansas and joined Lane's Jayhawkers. By 1858 he had been trained as a first-class soldier and was promoted to first lieutenant. All the while, his internal anger seethed as he waited to enact his revenge on these killers.

Quantrill now knew every detail of the workings on the inside of his Jayhawkers detachment. He began to methodically and deliberately ambush and kill each of his fellow soldiers who had been a part of the attack on him and his brother. He was able to murder, one by one, nearly everyone on his targeted list. Gradually suspicion as to who was committing the murders led to Quantrill, but by the time the Jayhawkers realized it was him, he had deserted the camp and fled to southern Missouri. There he organized a band of guerrillas to carry on the fight against the Kansans. The group would number about 350 men.

Sketch of Jim Clark that appeared in the *Rocky Mountain News*, August 8, 1895. *CO Historical Society*

Jim Clark had grown into a young man and had been kept informed of Quantrill's whereabouts. He was about eighteen years old when he left home and joined up with Quantrill's gang.

Jim learned how to handle a gun and was said to have become a crack shot. He was one of Quantrill's most reliable officers as the band joined in on the Confederate side to begin the Civil War in 1860. Clark was fearless in his fighting.

One story tells how he was casually riding his horse along a back road in Missouri when four northern cavalry men came into view heading toward him. They were out searching for any of Quantrill's guerrillas they could find. Jim Clark had to react fast, and with his bridle reins in his teeth he kicked his horse into full gallop charging head-on toward the soldiers. He held a revolver in each hand and blasted his guns at the men. All four federal soldiers were killed.

Thousands of young men were involved in the Civil War, and like Jim Clark, they became proficient in the use of a gun and grew hardened to the ways of killing. When the war was over, most soldiers returned home and went back to farming, but others could not give up the killing. Members of the infamous Quantrill guerrillas had included the later-to-be-outlaws, the James Brothers and the Younger Brothers.

William Quantrill died in a battle during the war. Jim Clark decided to join up with Jesse James and the Youngers, and went on to robbing banks and holding up stages and trains. Not too much is known about this period of Jim's life. He may have alternately worked jobs as well as engaged in outlaw activities. There are no facts about whether he was ever married. He would later be known as a man who had no interest in women and who particularly disliked prostitutes. It might be surmised that he had had a bad experience in romance, possibly with a prostitute, but no one knows for sure what may have happened.

Eventually he would drift away from the gang and head west. In the 1870s and 1880s, Leadville, Colorado was a wild silver boomtown, and Clark got a job there as a miner. He was already a large man, but this job's physical labor made him very strong.

Leadville attracted all kinds of entertainment for the miners. Many of them had hard-earned money from the ore they dug, and there was no shortage of people who were hoping to get them to spend it. One event brought a world champion heavyweight prizefighter to town. A hundred-dollar bill was offered to any man who could stay standing for five minutes in the ring with the boxer. The huge crowd would then place bets on their choice for winner. Jim Clark accepted the challenge. He stayed on his feet for the required five minutes while he did his best to box against the skilled fists of the trained fighter. Although he won the prize money, he told a friend later that "it was the hardest hundred bucks he had ever earned."

It is suspected that Clark participated in some of the holdups and other crimes around Leadville in those years. He knew Luke Short, a local bandit, and was rewarded with part of the proceeds from one of

Luke's stage robberies after loaning out his double-barreled shotgun for the occasion.

Clark arrived in Telluride in 1887. He took a job digging a pipeline and made a little cabin his home. It didn't take him long to find out that the town was lawless. The marshal was afraid to stand up to the drunken ruffians who shot up the town every night.

Clark approached the mayor with an offer to tame the lawless element. The mayor was weary of the town hoodlums and thought Clark looked like he might be able to help. He made Clark deputy marshal on the spot. That very night, Telluride experienced the first peace and quiet it had in a long time, and Clark didn't even have to use his guns. His physical prowess alone overcame the rowdy gunmen, and when they started to draw their guns, Clark knocked them down with his fists.

Beginning the next morning, Deputy Jim Clark was made Marshal Jim Clark. Thus began several years of peace in Telluride. Clark wouldn't stand for any disorderliness or misconduct in town. He never partook of liquor. One of his favorite sayings about alcoholics was, "Old John Barleycorn will beat them every time."

But there were rumors that he continued a lawless life outside of town. Some suspected Clark of dressing in disguise and robbing people along the trails leading from Telluride. Others believed he would tip off his outlaw acquaintances about gold and silver shipments headed out of town on the stage. Then he would get a cut of the booty.

On June 24, 1889 at about noon, three men rode into Telluride and steered their horses in front of the San Miguel County bank. While one of them stayed behind to hold the horses, the other two walked in and demanded all the cash from the assistant cashier. Within minutes, the outlaws had scooped up all the money, cleaned out the safe, and were back on their horses racing down Main Street. They shot their six-shooters in the air and whooped and hollered all the way out of town. Telluride's bank had just been robbed by Butch Cassidy, Tom McCarty, and Matt Warner. Marshal Clark later said that he'd received $2,200 for staying away from town that day.

Meanwhile, throughout the years he was in Telluride, he was also enforcing the law. He helped Sheriff Cyrus Wells "Doc" Shores of Gunnison round up cattle rustlers who had stolen part of a local rancher's herd. In return, Doc aided Clark if needed. They began quite a friendship, and whenever Shores was in Telluride, he would stop in and stay overnight with Clark.

Clark always patrolled the town each evening and he invited Doc to come along one night. They passed through the bordello area where one of the madams came outside with her dog. She said her dog was very old, and asked Clark if he would sometime take the dog out of town and put it out of its misery. The marshal pulled out his revolver and promptly shot the dog right there. He walked on without acting like anything had happened and said in disgust: "I don't even like to talk to [those women]." It left Doc to wonder what might have happened in Clark's past to elicit this comment.

Marshal Clark also took special interest in helping the needy and elderly of the town. He sometimes helped them with their chores and made repairs on their shacks. He generously lent money to destitute families. Perhaps this is how he justified making money from robberies or holdups.

Sheriff Doc Shores was with Clark one evening when they spotted a small boy struggling to drag two camp kettles full of water up an embankment. Clark hastened over to help him carry the water to his mother's cabin, where she eked out a living as a washerwoman. He didn't stop there though. He also saw to it that the family got an old horse to pull the water up the hill, using a whiskey barrel that Clark had helped rig.

One day, Clark took quick aim with his gun at a robin up in a tree. He seemed to be playing and not really wanting to kill the bird, but the bird was wounded and it fluttered and made a loud whining sound. Jim

Clark was obviously upset by this, and said to his friend: "You know Doc, that was a crazy thing to do—shooting such a defenseless little thing as a robin."

Yet, the other side of Marshal Clark would surface again. One evening he showed Doc the disguise he had hidden under a floorboard in his cabin. He admitted that this was what he wore when he robbed miners bringing in their ore. Clark said they "throw it away in some saloon or sporting house. I can put the money to much better use." Then Clark said it was kind of humorous to have these same fellows come into his office the next day to report the robbery to him.

Clark also had friends in the gambling houses whom he helped out in various ways. They paid him off with money on the side. Clark said, "It sort of helps supplement my salary as marshal."

Doc never told anyone about these "side businesses" of Clark's, but it troubled him. Of course he liked Clark, and he also saw the truly benevolent side of him. Overall, Clark had done more for Telluride than anyone else had ever done before. Some of the stories about Clark's other life were already rumored in town, and Doc did not think it was his place to interfere.

In 1894 Doc was in Delores, Colorado preparing to escort a prisoner to the state penitentiary in Cañon City. The convict had held up the railroad station in Mancos and Doc had testified against him, helping secure a "guilty" verdict from the jury. Clark had come from Telluride to help him, because he was concerned Doc was in danger of being ambushed. The local outlaw element had previously prevented law enforcement from interfering with their operations. Doc Shores could not be "bought" and was a serious threat to them.

One man, who was in a drunken stupor, was challenging Doc at the station. He had harassed Doc and Clark again and again, and Clark was ready to shoot him. Doc wanted to get out of town without the additional complications of having to return for a hearing if the man was killed. Clark restrained himself only in deference to Doc's request.

Finally, as the man became even more intolerable, Clark shouted that he would beat him up. The drunken man realized the power of Clark and decided not to push it any further. They got out of town peacefully, but Doc Shores always thought it was only because of Clark.

Although Telluride owed a lot to Clark for keeping the derelicts under control, the town council had grown tired of hearing all the rumors of his criminal deeds. They knew many were true. The evidence against Clark had become too damaging for them to overlook, so they decided to secretly look for his replacement. It was not easy to find someone who would stand up to the rowdy element like Clark did, but a deputy had been hired to help Clark cover the night shift. His name was MacDuff and although he had been hired to assist Clark, he soon established himself as capable enough to fill Clark's shoes.

The town council fired Clark and promoted MacDuff to city marshal. Jim Clark's reaction was not only angry, it was vengeful. Doc Shores was sent for by the local judge and was asked to come and try to calm down Clark. Threats had been made against the town council members, and Clark had already assaulted the new night deputy.

Doc said he would try his best to help, but didn't think Jim would listen to him. The judge said he was afraid somebody was going to get hurt if Jim couldn't be talked into leaving town. Doc was worried too. He visited Jim at his cabin and decided to stay overnight there. In the morning Doc told Jim he was concerned for his safety. He said the town officials wanted Jim gone, one way or the other. He warned Jim of a possible bushwhack yet Jim would not leave.

Jim Clark seemed shocked that all this was happening to him and didn't even want to talk about it. But he finally said he would like to be a marshal again somewhere. He asked if Shores would write him a letter of recommendation, which of course Doc agreed to do.

As soon as Doc returned home to Gunnison, he wrote the letter Jim had requested. He had no trouble singing the praises of his friend, and then he sent the letter to Jim. Only a day or two later, Doc received a telegram from the county clerk saying Jim Clark had been killed. It requested that Doc come if he could.

After Doc arrived on the train the next evening, he was told what had happened. Jim Clark had been walking down Main Street around midnight. He was with a man called Mexican Sam. A shot rang out and Clark was hit. The bullet went through Clark's chest and out his back. An artery was severed and he bled to death in less than an hour. Jim Clark died on August 6, 1895. He was fifty-four years old. Nearly the whole town of Telluride attended the funeral. In spite of his contradictory nature, he was remembered for establishing law and order there.

Doc wrote his memoirs many years later, in which he admitted that he went to Jim's cabin after the funeral and pulled up the floorboard. He removed the clothing Jim had used as a disguise in all the robberies of the local miners. Then he burned them.

Lou Blonger, Overlord of the Underworld

It was the year 1922 when Harry Tammen, called the "Little Dutchman," who co-published the *Denver Post*, said to one of his reporters: "You know, son, I'm sure sorry we had to print old Lou's name, but the story got so damn big we simply couldn't hold it out any longer."

Tammen was referring to one of the biggest stories in the news business and in Denver history. Lou Blonger had been arrested that day and his crimes were finally exposed and out in the open. Up until then, Lou had managed to befriend all the "right" people in Denver, and he kept his name separate from his underworld activities. Apparently, even the *Denver Post* had not felt the need to make too much of Blonger's "business," because it seemed harmless enough. Except to the victims. Blonger had spent years doing one thing very well, and that was to "catch a sucker." But on this day, his underworld and con game racket finally "caught" him.

Lou Blonger was short, rotund, and likeable. His main physical characteristics were his large bulbous nose and protruding lower lip. At the theatre and other public events he enjoyed wearing full formal dress, which drew attention in a crowd.

His working life in Denver started in the saloon business in 1880. He was a French-Canadian who had previously operated a few illegal activities in New Orleans and Salt Lake City. He had also run a Denver dance hall.

Blonger branched out into the gambling business with the policy shop racket. "Policy" was considered the poor man's gambling game, because it made the poor even poorer. It was similar to the numbers racket, which paid off for picking the winning number. Like all numbers games, the odds were highly stacked against the bettor, but the reward for winning was very enticing. A "day number" paid five to one if any number up to seventy-eight was among the first fifteen numbers drawn. Or a bettor could win thirty-two to one if his two selected numbers, called a "saddle," appeared anywhere on the list. A "station number" paid sixty to one if the winning number was in a specific position on the list. Blonger soon became the kingpin of Denver's policy shop racket.

When Lou Blonger arrived in Denver, Doc Baggs was already operating a con scheme that swindled men out of thousands of dollars at a time. Baggs donned a glossy stovepipe hat and carried a silk umbrella wherever he went. He could never understand why another Denver con-game newcomer, Soapy Smith, settled for cheating a sucker out of five dollars when he could have conned him for so much more.

Doc Baggs was growing old and Soapy Smith had begun to dominate Denver's confidence racket, forcing Doc to join his gang. Soapy was interested in fast profits in mass volume. Lou Blonger was soon forced to join with Soapy too, if he wanted to run his schemes in Denver. Lou would eventually take Doc's technique and develop it into a multimillion-dollar racket. Soapy later left Denver for Creede, Colorado, and when he returned a few years later, it would be Blonger who demanded and received a percentage of Soapy's profits. Lou Blonger had become the leader of Denver's underworld, and every other con man had to report to him.

Blonger had learned a lot from Soapy in the early days. Just as Soapy had done, he and the members of his growing underworld group preyed only on visitors to Denver, not the local residents. Blonger also maintained protection from local law enforcement by contributing heavily to both parties during election time. His payroll included many highly ranked officials in the police department, district attorney's office, and the local office of the U.S. Department of Justice.

The summer tourist season was one of the best times for Blonger to operate his new scheme. He had learned it from Doc Baggs who liked to make thousands of dollars off of each "sucker." One of Blonger's men, called a "steerer," would stand near the newsstands waiting for a prosperous looking man to buy an out-of-town newspaper. He would then follow the man back to his hotel lobby and wait for an opportunity to sit next to him for a moment. Then the steerer would get up and walk away, leaving a wallet on his vacated seat.

The out-of-town stranger, seeing the wallet, would pick it up and look inside for information about the owner so the wallet could be returned. The stranger would find a ten-dollar bill, a newspaper clipping, and a document. The clipping told of a huge profit made in a stock-market transaction by a man whose picture was shown. There was also a $100,000 bond, which guaranteed his ability to provide this service. The clipping and bond were both forgeries.

Usually the stranger would turn in the wallet at the hotel's front desk. The next day, the steerer would come to the hotel to claim the "lost" wallet. He would be accompanied by another man called the "spieler." The grateful owner of the wallet would ask the hotel clerk where he might find the person who had returned it. He and the spieler would then meet the out-of-town stranger to thank him. The stranger, now dubbed the "sucker" by the con men, would immediately recognize the owner of the wallet as the man whose picture was in the newspaper clipping.

The steerer would graciously thank the sucker and expound on the importance of the bond in his market transactions. He would then offer the sucker a reward for finding the wallet and its contents. The spieler would then go into action by interrupting this offer saying: "From his appearance, this gentleman obviously is not the type who would accept a cash reward. Why don't you show your appreciation by giving him a tip on the market? Give him a chance to make some money."

The steerer would mildly object to this idea, saying he wasn't supposed to give out tips, but, on the other hand, he was indebted to this

Lou Blonger was finally imprisoned at the age of seventy-three.
Denver Public Library, Western History Collection, Z-8995

man who had returned his bond. The spieler would then take over by lauding the abilities of the stock market operator. He would relate how he'd seen him make thousands of dollars in the last thirty days. He said that he had cleaned up on a couple thousand as the result of a tip he'd been given by this talented man. The clincher in the spiel was when he told the sucker that he was sending for more money from his relatives back in his hometown, so that he could get into the next big deal. It was expected to bring a huge return within the next few weeks. This suggestion was to encourage the sucker to think about what a "sure thing" this must be if the man would do that.

The sucker usually showed interest since he had seen for himself the newspaper clipping and the $100,000 bond to back up the stock operator's abilities. He was offered an opportunity to go with the two men the next day to visit the stock exchange. The sucker had nothing to lose by taking a look, so he agreed to meet them. Little did the sucker know that the "stock exchange" was a complete fake, created specifically to lure him in for the kill.

The stock exchange looked entirely real to the sucker, and he would overhear the stock operator say that he had just made a profit that morning. He had earned thousands of dollars when his stock had gone up two points. Then he predicted that it was likely to double in a few weeks, so he decided to leave his cash in this stock a while longer rather than cash out his profit.

The spieler, who also overheard this remark, would lean toward the sucker and start talking to him in a low voice. He would say: "This is too good a chance to lose. Let's go in together and make a killing."

The spieler would then buy a few thousand dollars of stock while the sucker watched. No further pressure was put on him, and they would all leave the stock exchange, inviting the sucker to accompany them again the next day. The next day their visit would be rewarded by more good news that the stock had gone up again. With this good news as encouragement, the sucker would then place a minimal buying order, putting up no cash. Each day they came back to find the stock had continued to rise. When the stock appeared to have tripled, the spieler suggested they sell and take their winnings. The cashier would actually place a huge stack of cash in the sucker's hands before realizing that the customer had not originally made a payment. The cash was pulled back by the cashier who would say: "Our customers must either establish a line of credit or put up the actual cash." He would add, "It's merely a formality, as soon as you produce the cash as evidence of good faith, we'll settle the account."

The sucker had seen the money in his hands and believed he only needed to come up with the cash to be rewarded with triple that amount. The spieler, who had also supposedly bought a large amount of stock, then suggested that the sucker go back home to get the needed cash. He was even encouraged to mortgage his house if necessary to get the money. The sucker would go home to raise the cash and return to meet the spieler. Then they both went together to the stock exchange and the sucker presented the cash. The cashier would say that everything was now in order, and that they should return the next day to receive their winnings.

Unfortunately, they were told the next day that the stock price had plummeted overnight and they had both lost all their money. The spieler would be outraged over this information and would start a fight with the cashier, even taking a swing at him with his fist. The brawl would be broken up, and the spieler and the sucker would leave empty handed. The spieler would try to console the sucker, who believed they both had been big losers.

Usually the sucker was never aware that he had been a victim of a confidence game. The spieler's final task was to get the sucker out of town. He was advised to go home and wait while the spieler promised he would try to get their money back somehow. Nothing would ever come of it, though, and the sucker would often be too ashamed to admit his loss. If he did suspect the scam, his pride usually prevented him from admitting he had been such a sucker. Either way, the con men were rarely reported.

If the ruse was reported by a victim, the police first tipped off Blonger, who would vacate the stock exchange location before the police arrived. The victim was then victimized once again by being made to look like a fool when he led the police to an empty office.

Lou Blonger's gang is said to have swindled countless men out of a total of $645,720 in one season. Another account suggests the figure was as high as one million dollars. The typical victim was suckered for around $5,000, but it could range as high as $100,000 depending on his wealth. By 1920, only one gang member was ever tried and convicted for this crime.

Blonger, in his early seventies, had enjoyed decades of success in maintaining a stronghold over his Denver operations. He was said to have had additional branches of his racket operating in Florida, California, and Havana.

He planned to continue to run his operation in Denver with the blessings of the corrupt officials. His mob did all the work, and he maintained the relationship with politicians by paying them off handsomely. A direct phone line was said to have been installed between Blonger and the chief of police.

What Blonger hadn't counted on was an honest district attorney. Philip S. Van Cise ran for the office in 1920. He had been a colonel in World War I and he was a popular candidate among Denver citizens. Blonger tried his usual approach and offered Van Cise a $25,000 campaign donation. If elected, all Blonger wanted in return was for Van Cise to fix the bonds at $1,000 for any of his mob who might be arrested.

Not only did Van Cise turn down the offer, he won the election, and immediately began to lay plans to bring down Blonger. It would take fifteen months of preparation while he used special investigators, hidden dictaphones, and records gathered from victims of the gang from across the country. In one neatly planned operation, a surprise raid was about to end Lou Blonger's criminal career.

It began at dawn on August 14, 1922 when Van Cise gave the signal to begin the ambush of the entire Blonger gang, numbering sixty-three members. Deputies, special deputies, and members of the state ranger force began their carefully designed actions.

One by one and in twos and threes, the gang members were quietly rounded up by the various deputies and rangers. Many were found at their homes, apartments, and other lodgings. Others were eating breakfast at local cafes and some had just emerged onto the streets. They were not taken to the local city and county jails. If they had been, the whole operation would have been given away as soon as the first prisoner entered. Van Cise had thought of this in advance, and obtained permission to use the Universalist Church as a temporary holding place. Lou Blonger was among the first to be brought in, and all of the men were stripped and searched.

One startling side event almost undermined the whole scheme that Van Cise led that day. He had been painstakingly precise in every part of his strategy to get Blonger and his mob. However, he could not have accounted for an overzealous *Denver Post* reporter who picked up a tip the night before the raid. The lucky part for Van Cise is that the reporter didn't know for whom the raid was intended. The reporter's information suggested it would take place at the statehouse, so he showed up at the Capitol building at daylight. He ran across various deputies, who were leaving to get into their cars, but none of them would talk to him. He had overheard an earlier conversation by one of the officers that mentioned a church. He repeated this about a "church" to see if it got any attention. One of the officers heard him and feared that the reporter knew far more than he really did and offered to take him there, hoping to detain him. At the Universalist Church the reporter still did not realize what was happening until he recognized Lou Blonger being led into the building. Immediately he ran for a phone, but was blocked by a guard. Events were soon transpiring so quickly that the guard left the reporter unattended. He got away and was able to phone in the story to the *Post*.

Another lucky break for Van Cise came when the reporter returned and shamelessly announced he had called the *Post*. The district attorney had just enough time to call the managing editor to convince him to hold the story. The editor agreed to hold it rather than ruin the raid. Although the young reporter lost his big scoop, the story was printed and ran the next day. Lou Blonger had always managed to keep his name out of the newspapers, but this time Harry Tammen said they had to run it.

About thirty-four gang members were captured that day. Of those, twenty actually went to trial in Denver. A few were turned over to officials in other states. Six jumped their bond, and one was declared insane.

Lou Blonger and his chief assistant, Adolph W. Duff, alias "Kid Duffy," spent large parts of their fortunes to defend themselves. Legions of attorneys were hired contending that the state could not prove its case against them. The two men were confident that they would be acquitted when the trial began in February of 1923.

Van Cise had done his homework, however, and the time spent on investigating Blonger, Duff, and the other con men paid off when all the evidence was presented to the jury. It took the jury four days to reach a guilty verdict. Blonger and Duff were sent to prison for seven years each. The other defendants received three years. Since Lou Blonger was already seventy-three years old, seven years turned out to be longer than he could survive. He died in prison, and so did an era of organized crime in Denver.

Citizens Save Their Bank from Robbers

In mid-October of 1896, telling headlines popped up in newspapers all over Colorado. The October 16 *Rocky Mountain News* caption read: "Meeker's Dead Robbers." The next day, the Grand Junction *Weekly Star-Times* banner told its version: "Filled Them With Lead." The same day, the Colorado Springs *Gazette* hailed: "Desperadoes Were At Work." Days later, follow-up articles decried, "A Pathetic Incident," in the *Rocky Mountain News,* and "The Robbers Identified," in the Grand Junction *Weekly Star-Times.* All the articles were reported from Meeker, Colorado.

Meeker was a small, isolated town situated in the northwestern part of the state along the western slope of the Rocky Mountains. October was historically not a good month for this place. Seventeen years earlier in October of 1879, Indian Agent Nathan C. Meeker and several other agency employees had been killed by Utes in a skirmish which came to be called "The Meeker Massacre." Spelling the beginning of the end for Ute occupation of this land, they were soon marched off to reservations in Utah and southern Colorado in 1881. The town was eventually established near the agency site and named in honor of the dead agent.

By 1896, Meeker boasted a Main Street with several side streets crossing it. There was a mercantile store owned by J. W. Hugus, with the Bank of Meeker located in the store at the far end of the building. The store and bank were located at Sixth and Main Street. Wagon sheds were located next to the store.

Also by this time, the infamous group of outlaws called the Wild Bunch, led by Butch Cassidy, often used a hide-out at Brown's Park,

The J. W. Hugus building housed the mercantile store and the Bank of Meeker, 1896.
CO Historical Society, #G15805

Colorado, sometimes called Brown's Hole. It was northwest of Meeker in a beautiful valley along the Green River. It also sat alongside the Outlaw Trail, which served as a rugged pathway for renegades running up and down the western slope from Canada to Mexico. Four young men from Brown's Park championed the Wild Bunch as their heroes, and called themselves the "Junior Wild Bunch." Ripe to prove their veracity, they rode into Meeker on October 13, 1896.

It was about 2:30 in the afternoon when three of the young men walked into the Meeker Mercantile Store. Their horses had been tied up at the wagon shed next door. Two came in the front door and one came through a side door. The fourth remained at the edge of town with fresh horses ready for the get-away.

Joe Rooney was a clerk at the Meeker Hotel and had just arrived at the bank to make a deposit. The assistant cashier, David Smith, talked with him while taking care of Rooney's business. Just as Rooney was ready to leave, he and Smith were confronted by one of the young men holding a gun in their faces. "Hands up," he said to Smith.

Smith was startled and didn't react immediately. The impatient gunman fired a warning shot past the side of his head. When Smith's reaction was still frozen, another shot was fired past him. Finally coming to his senses, Smith immediately raised his hands.

The other two gunmen had by now taken charge of the customers and store employees. These folks were directed to the center of the room where the robbers disarmed them. The robbers also took other guns and ammunition from the store shelves.

Outside on Main Street, Deputy Game Warden W. H. Clark was the first to hear the sound of gunfire coming from the store and bank. This was the first mistake of the Junior Wild Bunch, since the warning shots they fired inside the bank at Smith also warned the entire town of Meeker.

Meanwhile, the robbers demanded the money from the bank's safe. The head cashier, a man named Moulton, was summoned from a side room and held at gunpoint while he opened it. Seven hundred dollars in cash was in the safe's drawer. The robber quickly scooped it up and stashed it in a sack. All of this took place in a few short minutes with only a few words spoken. Mostly it was eerily silent as the robbery took place.

The three young robbers now instructed all the people in the store and bank to walk out the side door in single file. The robbers would be right behind them with the crowd acting as a buffer in case there was any trouble. Once outside, they planned to mount their horses and make a run for the edge of town where the fresh horses were being held for them.

Little did they know that the town of Meeker had been organizing the robbers' "welcoming committee" while they had been inside the bank. Deputy Game Warden Clark had immediately surmised that a robbery was underway when he'd heard the shots. He also saw the horses tied by the wagon sheds on the side of the store. It was a pretty safe bet that the robbers would exit from that side door.

Several men had been hastily gathered by Clark and were posted outside the side and front doors of the store and bank. They had pistols, rifles, and shotguns. All they had to do was hide themselves behind some barrels and sheds, and wait.

The customers, clerks, and bank employees began to parade out the side door. Some were immediately aware that their fellow citizens were set for an ambush when they saw a few gun barrels projecting out from behind nearby barriers. None gave even a hint of what they saw, leading the robbers right out the door and into the trap. Then they scattered for cover.

The first robber who came out the side door saw the now uncon-cealed citizens as they stood up and aimed their guns directly at him. It probably never crossed his mind to stop and surrender right on the spot. This was the gang's second mistake. The man's self-defense reflex kicked in and he fired his newly stolen rifle at the first man in his sights. It was Clark, who was shot in the left side of his chest, barely missing his lung. The other two robbers were right behind the first and instinctively pulled their guns and also started shooting. Simultaneously, all the Meeker citizens fired back at the robbers with bullets coming from all directions.

When the smoke cleared, two robbers lay dead, wounded several times by various shots that left holes throughout their bodies. The third robber, who turned out to be the youngest, also was struck several times. Somehow, he remained standing and continued forward before he fell at the corner of Sixth Street and Market.

He managed to stay alive for another hour and a half. He said his name was George Harris. He also identified the others who had been in the robbery with him. One was Charles Jones and the other was William Smith. The young hoodlum's last words were, "Oh, Mother!"

The fourth member of the gang heard the commotion and gunshots ringing out in the town. When his partners didn't show up right away, he made a run for it back to Brown's Hole.

Other Meeker citizens were also wounded in the melee. Besides Clark's wound—which he survived—Victor Dikeman was shot in the arm, C. A. Booth's scalp was grazed near his ear, and W.P. Herrick's finger was shot off.

Several days later, two men arrived in Meeker from Brown's Hole. They took charge of the horses left by the robbers and identified the bodies. It seems that the young robber who died last had protected himself and his buddies right to the end. His name was actually Billy Smith. The other two were George Law and Jim Shirley. Law was the nephew of a store owner in Brown's Hole and young Shirley was also a resident there. Billy was from Johnson County, Wyoming.

Photographs were taken of the bodies, which were then turned over to the undertaker. Justifiable homicide was the verdict at the inquest.

Meeker citizens chose to put the corpses on display for several days to serve as a lesson to any other possible criminals who might think Meeker was an easy target. For years the photographs of the bodies were put on permanent exhibition for all to see. Apparently it worked as a strong deterrent, since no bank robberies were attempted in Meeker for many years.

The Feminine Side

Few women ventured into early Colorado—a wild and lawless place in the late 1800s and into the 1900s. Those who did come were usually accompanied by their husbands. Unmarried, adventurous women often migrated here out of desperation but found limited opportunities. Crime was not often resorted to, but it was possibly more widespread than records show. The male majority was generally protective of women, even though they also sometimes mistreated them. Females who committed crimes were rarely arrested. If they were, they were rarely convicted and almost never imprisoned.

Three separate Colorado women, each with criminal motives involving a lover, fiancé, or husband, experienced various facets of what the law meted out for crimes committed by women. Only one went to jail.

Mattie Silks was a well-known madam residing in lower downtown Denver where she ran a parlor for men. Her love interest was Cort Thomson, often called the "handsome man."

Mattie and Cort had first met in Chicago around 1870. He was a foot racer who challenged competitors to running contests, while others bet on the winner. In his "pink tights and star spangled trunks," he held women breathless. After Mattie met him she immediately placed a bet on this slender, sandy-haired Texan to win. When he beat his opponent, Mattie walked away with her skirt held up to carry all of her winnings, and also with a new romantic partner.

Mattie and Cort reconnected later in Denver, where their bond remained strong. Mattie loved this handsome man, who earned little money by foot racing. Cort loved the becoming Mattie who earned plenty of income for both of them.

One sunny Denver afternoon in 1877, Cort raced against the note-worthy Sam Doherty in a 125-yard dash. The winner would take all, and Mattie bet $2,000 on Cort. When he nosed out Doherty for the win, Mattie decided to host an evening victory party with her winnings. All were invited for champagne at Denver's large dance hall the Olympic Gardens. It was said to be one of the wildest parties in an already notably wild town.

In attendance was a woman named Katie Fulton, a madam who ran a brothel just a block away from Mattie's place. Facts are uncertain about how the feud between Katie and Mattie developed that evening, but by all accounts, Cort was at the center of it. Mattie was angry enough to challenge Katie to a duel outside along the banks of the Platte River.

In what was likely one of the first pistol duels ever staged between women, Katie and Mattie marched off their paces from each other, turned around on the count of three, and aimed their guns at one another. After the shots were fired, only one person fell to the ground holding a bleeding neck. Not Mattie. Not Katie. It was Cort Thomson who lay wounded, though not mortally. Mattie ran to his side, nursed him, and later had him taken back to his quarters a block away from her establishment. From the angle which the bullet grazed Thomson's neck, it was obvious that Katie's gun had done the damage.

It was never known, or at least admitted to, if Katie Fulton was a bad shot or had, in fact, intended her erring bullet to hit the "cause" of this dispute. The ladies employed at the local men's parlors all felt certain Katie had planned to shoot Cort from the start. The *Rocky Mountain News* reported on the incident and the wild party, and spent several paragraphs remonstrating the authorities for allowing these activities.

Denver City leaders, some of whom were Mattie's and Katie's cus-tomers, breathed a sigh of relief when it was determined that the women's duel, the attempted murder, and the wild party had all taken

Mattie Silks made over a half million dollars from the world's oldest profession, but a good-for-nothing broke her heart

The Scarlet Lady

By FORBES PARKHILL

M SILKS

© Colorado Historical Society

Photographs from the collection of Fred M. Mazzula

This book cover shows a portrait of Mattie Silks, Denver Madam, in all her fashion finery. Her doorstep displayed her name in fancy tiles.
CO Historical Society, F32942

place just outside of the Denver city limits. The police would not have to make any arrests.

Jessie Landers had found work at Lake City's Crystal Palace dance hall and bordello in 1895. She was engaged to be married soon to twenty-two-year-old Louis Estep, the only son of his widowed mother.

Lake City was no longer booming. The mining of silver had been the area's main industry and the town had thrived on this foundation. When silver prices languished and ore became harder to find, the town population and businesses began to shrivel too. The Crystal Palace was still filled to capacity, but its success would soon come to an abrupt halt.

One evening Jessie Landers came out of her room at the Palace and saw Louis talking with a man named Frank McDonald. She did not like McDonald's reputation, and for some reason seeing him in conversation with her fiancé enraged Jessie. She pulled out a gun and aimed it at McDonald, who was standing in front of the door to the grand ballroom. Instead of hitting McDonald, the bullet struck Louis in the head behind his ear. Jessie then fired two more shots at McDonald as he ran from the scene. She missed him both times.

Louis Estep died instantly and Jessie must have immediately realized the tragedy of the situation. She ran outside and pointed the gun at herself, sending a bullet through her chest, which came out her side. Amazingly, Jessie survived.

She was arrested and went to trial for manslaughter. The madam of the Crystal Palace, Clara Ogden, sided with Jessie and circulated a petition in favor of giving Jessie the minimum sentence. The judge in the case gave a short speech on the perils accompanying the lives of women who worked as prostitutes. He commented on the nature of her crime and the tragedy of it.

After pleading guilty, Jessie Landers was convicted of voluntary manslaughter. She was sentenced to serve five years in the state penitentiary located at Cañon City. The Crystal Palace closed down, and Lake City became an even quieter place.

In 1911, **Gertrude Gibson Patterson** was charged in a Denver district court when she "wilfully, unlawfully, feloniously, with malice aforethought, shot and killed her husband thereby violating the peace, dignity, and security of the people of the State of Colorado."

In one of the more sensational trials of early Denver, the public seemed insatiable for all the facts surrounding this case. It had all the right ingredients to keep the five Denver newspapers frantically vying for the scoop on the latest details. Denver citizens wanted to know what could have caused this woman to shoot her husband four times in the back, in broad daylight? Entire pages were devoted to the trial and every piece of new information. The finer points began to emerge and the public formed their own opinions regarding Mrs. Patterson's guilt.

Gertrude Gibson Patterson was a thirty-one-year-old strikingly beautiful woman. She had recently moved to Denver to join her twenty-six-year-old husband, who was suffering from tuberculosis. He was recovering at the Agnes Memorial Sanitarium. "Gertie" had found a bungalow nearby so she could visit him there.

Gertie had been born to poor parents in Sandoval, Illinois in 1881. As a young girl of thirteen, she was allegedly asked to leave school for violating rigid moral rules. Shortly thereafter she eloped with a saloon-keeper and went with him to Chicago. Her father had her brought back home, but a later visit to her sister in St. Louis gave her a chance to run off to Chicago again.

This time she met Emil W. Strouss, a wealthy and elderly clothing manufacturer. He was impressed by young Miss Gibson and asked her parents' consent to act as her benefactor. They agreed and soon she was on her way to Europe with Strouss, traveling the continent. She spent four years at a school in Paris, France, learned to speak French fluently, and was exposed to all the style, fashion, jewelry, and social graces available.

Strouss and Gertie returned to Chicago, where he moved into the classy Standard Club, and she boarded at the pricey Auditorium Hotel. She had no apparent income other than what Strouss provided.

While ice skating at a local resort, Gertie—who was now twenty-five years old—met the young twenty-year-old Charles A. Patterson. He was a clerk for a printing firm and had limited financial means. They soon fell in love and were married in California at Carmel-by-the-Sea, where they also honeymooned, all financed by Gertie's money from Strouss.

They returned to Chicago and she finally told Charles about her connection to Strouss. Running low on funds, Gertie went with Strouss
ne of his business trips to serve as his interpreter. Charles
pneumonia, which led to tuberculosis, and he decided to go
dry climate to recover in a sanitarium.

cts of their lives together become murky at this point. Charles
demanded that she return to be with him in Denver. He had
s angry about her relationship with Strouss and jealous about
t be going on between them. Gertie maintained that Charles
the scenes, manipulating her to get as much money out of
ssible. She stated that Charles was demanding more and
r his lifestyle as a gentleman. Quarrels that had begun
rriage developed into Charles' abusiveness toward
had periodically slapped her, knocked her down, and
b lanned to divorce him when she discovered he had
fil s demanding $25,000 for "alienation of the affec-
tio

rial said that on the day of the murder, Gertie
calle anitarium and asked to meet with him privately. A
mutu ocation was decided upon and Charles left the san-
itariu efore the appointed time. A caretaker of a mansion next to
the park where Gertie and Charles met testified that he had heard them
quarreling. Gertie maintained that Charles began to hit her until she was
knocked to the ground. She admitted to pulling a gun from her purse
and shooting him. The gun was found at the scene.

It was Gertie's word of self-defense against a strong amount of evidence against her, including the murder weapon. "It's thirty for Gertie,"
proclaimed a cynical reporter as the trial was coming to a close.

Without warning, the defense attorney suddenly called an unknown
final witness to the stand. The prosecution was stunned. The man was
sworn in and proceeded to tell how he had stayed at a local hotel the

night before the murder. He had arrived from Wyoming and was just passing through. The next day he had decided to take a walk around town and as he neared the park, he saw a young couple talking excitedly about 300 feet away. This was followed by the spectacle of the man striking the woman, blow after blow, until she fell down. He then heard shots and saw the man go down. He claimed not to want any part of this at the time, so he walked quickly away. He identified Gertie as the woman he had seen that day. His final statement was, "But I saw enough. The woman's life was in danger!"

Then the jury was sent to its quarters to deliberate. They returned their verdict the next day. Gertrude Gibson Patterson was pronounced, "Not guilty." The prosecution was both outraged and incredulous stating: "If we couldn't convict a murderer on the evidence we presented, what is required in the way of truth and fact to convict?" One juror said the last witness had taken "the rope off [Gertie's] neck."

There was great suspicion about that last witness. One observer supposedly noticed him leaving his hotel after the trial with a large wad of cash. Another woman claimed that Gertie had received mail from Strouss during the trial, but no one could say what was in the letter and whether cash was included. A detective agency hired by the prosecution was never able to locate the man again.

Gertie Patterson left Denver for Europe. Her return voyage to America the following year was said to have been aboard a brand new ship, named . . . *The Titanic.*

Bibliography

Jack Slade

O'Dell, Roy Paul and Kenneth C. Jessen. *An Ear in His Pocket.* Loveland, Colorado: J.V. Publications, 1996.

Scott, Robert. *Slade! The True Story of the Notorious Badman.* Glendo, Wyoming: High Plains Press, 2004.

Southworth, Dave. *Feuds on the Western Frontier.* Round Rock, Texas: Wild Horse Publishing, 1999.

Twain, Mark. *Roughing It.* Hartford, Connecticut: American Publishing Company, 1872.

James Gordon

Casey, Lee, ed. *Denver Murders.* New York: Duell, Sloan, and Pearce, 1946.

Jessen, Kenneth. *Colorado Gunsmoke.* Boulder, Colorado: Pruett Publishing Company, 1986.

Perkin, Robert L. *The First One Hundred Years.* New York: Doubleday & Co., 1959.

Smiley, Jerome C. *History of Denver.* Denver: Old Americana Publishing Co., 1901.

The Espinosa Gang

Collier, William Ross and Edwin Victor Westrate. *Dave Cook of the Rockies*. New York: Rufus Rockwell Wilson, 1936.

Everett, George G. and Dr. Wendell F. Hutchinson. *Under the Angel of Shavano*. Denver: Golden Bell Press, 1963.

Kelsey, H. E. *Frontier Capitalist*. Boulder, Colorado: Pruett Publishing Company and State Historical Society of Colorado, 1969.

Simmons, Virginia McConnell. *The San Luis Valley*. Niwot, Colorado: University Press of Colorado, 1999.

Jim Reynolds

Collier, William Ross and Edwin Victor Westrate. *Dave Cook of the Rockies*. New York: Rufus Rockwell Wilson, 1936.

Drago, Harry Sinclair. *Lost Bonanzas*. New York: Bramhall House, 1966.

Everett, George G. and Dr. Wendell F. Hutchinson. *Under the Angel of Shavano*. Denver: Golden Bell Press, 1963.

Jessen, Kenneth. *Colorado Gunsmoke*. Boulder, Colorado: Pruett Publishing Company, 1986.

The Musgrove Gang

Collier, William Ross and Edwin Victor Westrate. *Dave Cook of the Rockies*. New York: Rufus Rockwell Wilson, 1936.

Jessen, Kenneth. *Colorado Gunsmoke.* Boulder, Colorado: Pruett Publishing Company, 1986.

Smiley, Jerome C. *History of Denver.* Denver: Old Americana Publishing Company, 1901.

Watrous, Ansel. *History of Larimer County.* Ft. Collins: Courier Printing and Publishing Company, 1911.

Ike and Port Stockton

Beckner, Raymond M. *Guns Along the Silvery San Juan.* Cañon City, Colorado: Master Printers, 1975.

Dugan, Mark. *Bandit Years.* Santa Fe, New Mexico: Sunstone Press, 1987.

McTighe, James. *Roadside History of Colorado.* Boulder, Colorado: Johnson Books, 1984.

Smith, Duane A. *Rocky Mountain Boom Town.* Albuquerque: University of New Mexico Press, 1980.

Alfred Packer

Gantt, Paul H. *The Case of Alfred Packer, the Man-Eater.* Denver: University of Denver Press, 1952.

Kushner, Ervan F. *Alferd G. Packer, Cannibal! Victim?* Frederick, Colorado: Platte 'N Press, 1980.

Kushner, Ervan F. *Otto Mears, His Life and Times with notes on Alferd Packer Case.* S. Platte: Jende-Hagan Book Corp., 1979.

Shores, Cyrus Wells. *Memoirs of a Lawman.* Denver: Sage Books, 1962.

"Soapy" Smith

Feitz, Leland. *Soapy Smith's Creede.* Colorado Springs: Little London Press, 1973.

McTighe, James. *Roadside History of Colorado.* Boulder, Colorado: Johnson Books, 1984.

Parkhill, Forbes B. *The Wildest of the West.* Denver: Sage Books, 1957.

Robertson, Frank C. and Beth Kay Harris. *Soapy Smith, King of the Frontier Con Men.* New York: Hastings House, 1961.

Jim Clark

Jessen, Kenneth. *Colorado Gunsmoke.* Boulder, Colorado: Pruett Publishing Company, 1986.

McTighe, James. *Roadside History of Colorado.* Boulder, Colorado: Johnson Books, 1984.

Shores, Cyrus Wells. *Memoirs of a Lawman.* Denver: Sage Books, 1962.

Lou Blonger

Parkhill, Forbes B. *The Wildest of the West.* Denver: Sage Books, 1957.

Citizens Save Their Bank from Robbers

Jessen, Kenneth. *Colorado Gunsmoke.* Boulder, Colorado: Pruett Publishing Company, 1986.

McTighe, James. *Roadside History of Colorado.* Boulder, Colorado: Johnson Books, 1984.

Patterson, Richard. *Historical Atlas of the Outlaw West.* Boulder, Colorado: Johnson Books, 1985.

Rockwell, Wilson. *Sunset Slope.* Denver: Bib Mountain Press, 1956.

The Feminine Side

Casey, Lee, ed. *Denver Murders.* New York: Duell, Sloan, and Pearce, 1946.

Jessen, Kenneth. *Colorado Gunsmoke.* Boulder, Colorado: Pruett Publishing Company, 1986.

Houston, Grant. *Lake City Reflections.* Gunnison, Colorado : B & B Printers, 1976.

Parkhill, Forbes B. *The Wildest of the West.* Denver: Sage Books, 1957.

Index

About the Author

J an Murphy was born in St. Louis, Missouri, to parents with the wanderlust, and had already gone on three Colorado vacations with them by the time she was eight years old. On these trips, she went to the top of Pikes Peak, built dams in the creek next to the family's cabin in Evergreen, and camped for two weeks in Rocky Mountain National Park.

Jan was thrilled when her family moved to Bear Creek Canyon in the Colorado mountains near Denver. She attended one of Colorado's last two-room schools, which had a real iron stove in the kitchen used to cook lunches. A few years later she rode the school bus down the canyon road every day to attend Red Rocks Jr. High School. The view from her classroom window was of the famed Red Rocks Park and Amphitheatre.

She attended Bear Creek High School and went on to college at the University of Colorado in Boulder. Her career took her to Washington D.C., New York and Boston, and she eventually returned to Colorado where she renewed her enjoyment of hiking. This included a five-day camping and hiking trip along a 55-mile segment of the Colorado Trail, led by Gudy Gaskill, the founder of the trail.

Jan has traveled throughout the United States, and to France, Luxembourg, and Mexico, but her favorite place is still Colorado. She taught Colorado history and hiking classes in local community education programs and at Lockheed Martin Astronautics Evening Institute for six years.

Now, writing about Colorado is her passion.